Contents

This volume contains the papers given at a weekend seminar at the Institute of Archaeology in London at Easter 1974. The subject was 'Burial in the Roman world' and the papers were all commissioned to try to live up to that title. To those who are not familiar with recent work on Roman burial, this selection of papers may need some explanation.

It was obvious that speakers could not be found in England who knew in detail all the provinces of the Empire, and their peculiarities of Roman burial. In retrospect this is extremely fortunate, for if those speakers had been found it is likely that everyone at the seminar (or reading this volume) would have had to submit to an endless catalogue of repetition incorporating minor details of regional variation. In place of full geographical coverage, therefore, we aimed to cover the methods and main areas of burial (regional, chronological, and special) and, more important, the methods being used to study the material.

Thus, for any survey of the Roman Empire a word is needed on the background in Italy from which the colonists and army of the centuries around the birth of Christ moved. This Glenys Davies undertook in a quick summary of published material. It shows the extreme complexity of the picture of burial in Italy, and the lack of uniformity. To complement this picture, John Collis undertook a survey of burial in north-west Europe before Rome influenced the burial customs of the Iron Age tribes. The spread of Roman burial customs and the rather surprising movement towards uniformity in burial in the Roman Empire is work still in progress, and here the need is for a survey of method rather than of the presently isolated groups of facts. Rick Jones, in a paper which was warmly discussed both favourably and unfavourably, suggests that the information is too great to be analysed by a human mind trying to remember the layout and goods of thousands of graves, a classical situation into which to introduce the abilities of the computer. Having made the general point he goes on to suggest a detailed method of the comparative analysis of graves anywhere and at any time.

The large cemetery is obviously the best source of knowledge for changing customs, so that the town cemetery is always assured of study. The small rural cemetery is equally deserving of study but, as John Collis shows, it has its own problems and its own opportunities for investigation. The site at Owslebury on which Dr Collis's remarks are based is at present being written up as a part of the general site report, but it is going to be some years before this is available. His paper here is therefore a trailer for future work, and, at the same time, more detailed analysis of the problems of the cemetery than will be possible in the final report.

The papers up to this point have been completely concerned with a purely material interpretation. Jock Macdonald's contribution takes us into the realm of theory and of belief. Since cemeteries are perhaps the best evidence we have of the beliefs of large numbers of the population concerning the after-life this perilous journey into what has been regarded as a lunatic fringe must be made; it is a tribute to the care with which Mr Macdonald planned his journey that there were few dissenters from his way of thought at the seminar.

In the later Empire the problem of distinct groups who have been recognized by their burial practice becomes acute, and we have taken two main examples, Germans and Christians. Malcolm Todd gives us a quick survey of the methods and customs of burial among the Free Germans outside the boundaries of the Empire. For the Christians, Christopher Green starts off in the cemetery which he has excavated at Poundbury, Dorchester, which he and many others regard as a Christian cemetery, and then follows the leads given there to the Rhineland and to North Africa, especially on the trail of plaster or gypsum burials.

A note on the help which can be obtained on the interpretation of burials from the literary sources leads to the final phase, in which Philip Rahtz follows the picture of Roman, and perhaps specifically Christian, burials into the 5th century and beyond. The Roman fashion has become the Christian fashion, and this becomes the standard medieval method of burial.

Only one lecture given at the seminar, that by Giles Clarke on the recognition of 'foreign' burials in the Lankhills cemetery at Winchester, has not been printed here. This is because it is the only paper which will be published in full elsewhere, and also the only cemetery report which is at present in the press. It will appear as Volume III, part 2, of *Winchester Studies*, and in that volume will be found a useful bibliography which will guide the reader or researcher into the field of late Roman burial in the western provinces of the Empire.

This whole question of population movement, recognition of burial rite, and the establishment of 'native' and 'intrusive' practices is, with Dr Clarke's work, firmly established in Britain. There is at present a gap on the continent, especially in Gaul, but also on the Rhine and Danube frontiers. The continental material to date is mainly aimed towards synthesis, and in that sense the continent is better served than Britain. The next step, however, is to attempt some fairly wide-ranging analysis of burial customs, as shown by large cemeteries, so that foreign influences, indigenous changes, and divergence of native practices may be defined and understood. This volume serves to highlight just this gap, of late Roman furnished cemeteries from which the better known cemeteries of the Migration period must presumably evolve.

Finally, a word is necessary about the policy of editing that has been followed. Most of the editing was done at the seminar when the fields of study were divided up and duplication avoided. Apart from that, only minor changes of wording have been made. The system of references and the illustrations are the choice of each author. This is not an unfortunate piece of laziness on the part of the editor, it is an essential part of the information communicated by each paper. Further, this is a challenge to those dull little grey men who mutter about uniformity, as an escape from individuality. There is virtue, and information, in variety; let those who disagree, instead of holding the field through lack of challenge, be made to demonstrate the superiority of their repressive way of thinking.

Pre-Roman burial rites in north-western Europe

John Collis

Introduction

Prehistory has been divided into two main modes, periods of living and periods of dying. The Iron Age is no exception. British archaeologists are familiar with the mysterious lack of burials which should accompany the Woodbury Culture, but the disappearing dead are no peculiarly insular problem, and though we in these islands gaze in envy at the wealth of burials that are found on 'the continent', we should not be oblivious of the fact that certain areas such as western and central France are equally graveless. On the other hand, in the areas where cemeteries are densest, occupation sites are usually rare and uninformative, and the British settlement evidence is without parallel anywhere on the continent in its richness and completeness.

Though I shall survey briefly the main developments of the burial rites in the La Tène Culture Group of Europe, geographically I shall mainly restrict myself to the areas which became Roman provinces in the one and a half centuries which started with Caesar's conquest of Gaul. To the great burial province of the Germanic cultures of the North European Plain I shall merely allude where there is enlightenment or contact with the areas to the south. Equally I shall be primarily concerned with the Late La Tène period, Déchelette II/III and Reinecke C/D. There is, however, one problem: some Late La Tène burials certainly post-date the Roman conquest, especially in Gaul, and at present our chronologies are not sufficiently refined to distinguish between pre- and post-conquest graves. It is not until about 15 BC with the foundation of such forts as Dangstetten (Fingerlin 1971) that we can really trust our chronology. Indeed, until fairly recently it was generally accepted that the main type of Late La Tène brooch, the Nauheim, was entirely post-Caesarean in date (Werner 1955), and Mahr (1967) could even argue that the rite of cremation burial in flat cemeteries was only introduced into the Trier area at the time of the Roman conquest.

But such depressed chronologies are no longer acceptable (Collis 1975b). The absence of the Nauheim brooch from the Alesia battlefield, the key-point for a low chronology, can now be explained, as this brooch seems to be purely a female ornament and therefore not to be expected in a military context. In any case all the bronze brooches supposed to be from Alesia are typologically later. The Nauheim brooch has now appeared stratified within or beneath ramparts which should be dateable to the Caesarean period at the latest, at Berne-Engehalbinsel (Müller Beck and Ettlinger 1962-3) and at Chateaumeillant (Gourvest 1956), and it may well go back a generation earlier. It also continues as late as mid-Augustan times, as demonstrated by grave 44 at the Titelberg in Luxembourg (Thill 1969). However we shall not be far wrong in assigning most burials with Nauheim brooches to the decade or two either side of 55 BC.

Burial rites of the La Tène period

In the areas with which we are concerned, three great modes of burial rites can be detected:

I   The earliest group belongs primarily to Reinecke A (475-400 BC). The body is usually inhumed under a barrow, though in some areas such as southern Bohemia cremation occurs. Throughout the area there is a minority of rich or very rich burials, some with imported Mediterranean goods, two-wheeled vehicles, and gold ornaments of local manufacture, decorated in La Tène art style. Weapons occur but are rare. These burials are found in the highland areas rich in metal ores and other resources (Driehaus 1965) (Fig. 1), extending in an arc from the Dürrnberg in Austria (Penninger 1973) in the east, through southern Bohemia (Filip 1956; fig. 80), Northern Bavaria (Kersten 1933), Thuringia, Hesse, the Hunsrück-Eifel (Joachim 1968), eastern France, and so down to the Côte d'Or and the central Loire (Déchelette 1914). Poorer burials occur in southern Bohemia in cemeteries (Šaldová 1955, Soudská 1968), but elsewhere they usually occur as multiple inhumations under barrows. Though some of the poorer burials continue into Reinecke B, the metal types characteristic of that period are generally absent. The rich burials also disappear, the one exception being the famous grave at Waldalgesheim.

II   The second mode is that of the flat cemeteries of Reinecke B-C (Filip 1956, 1960). The normal burial rite is extended inhumation in a flat grave, but at an early date cremations occur, especially in the east, and this becomes more common later on. The men are often buried with their weapons—sword, spear, shield and knife—and the women with their jewelry—brooches, bracelets, anklets and torcs. Rich burials with gold and silver or imported goods do not occur, and if there is a gold object it is only a finger ring or some such small item. In contrast to group I burials, these have a lowland distribution orientated towards the lighter agricultural soils such as loess and gravel (Fig. 2). Generally like Nebringen (Krämer 1964) they are small (up to 20-30 burials) and short-lived, and the long-lived cemetery at Münsingen is most exceptional (Hodson 1968). The distribution extends from the central Rhine valley and the Wetterau, Switzerland and the Alpine valleys, along the Danube into Hungary and Romania, north to southern Moravia, northern Bohemia, and parts of southern Poland. Geographically in central Europe these burials have almost no overlap with group I. In Switzerland some of the cemeteries start as early as Reinecke A, but elsewhere they do not occur until Reinecke B, typified by the Dux and Münsingen types of brooches. The later burials contain brooches of Middle La Tène construction, decorated with bosses on the foot, the latest being the Mötschwil or Moravian type with a small boss (Hodson 1968; Čizmář 1970).

I/II   There is one area which is an exception to the two groups defined above, the area of Champagne, and especially the Marne. Flat inhumations with weapons of the general type described appear in the Jogassian Culture of Hallstatt D, as do richer burials with four-wheeled vehicles. The cemeteries continue into Early La Tène, some being unusually large with up to 200 burials, but interspersed with these poorer burials are rich burials comparable to the group I burials with two-wheeled vehicles and imported goods, such as La Gorge Meillet and Somme Bionne. Champagne is also a lowland area

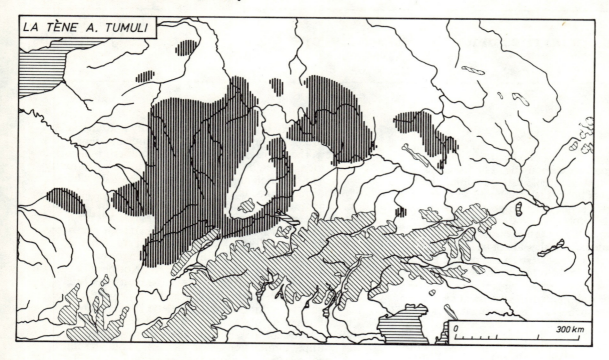

1   *Generalized distribution of tumulus burials of La Tène A*

lacking in mineral wealth, so the rich burials are doubly anomalous. With the Champagne burials must be linked the generally poorer and more problematical burials of the Arras Group of eastern Yorkshire (Stead 1965).

III   The third mode in burial custom I shall call here the North Gallic Culture, and it will be considered in greater detail below. It is characterized by cemeteries of

cremation burials in which pottery predominates among the grave-goods, though of metalwork brooches are quite common. It may start as early as the end of Reinecke C, but is mainly Reinecke D/Déchelette III, and continues into the Roman period. It extends from the central Rhine, across northern France and Belgium to south-eastern England. Rich burials occur throughout the area, with

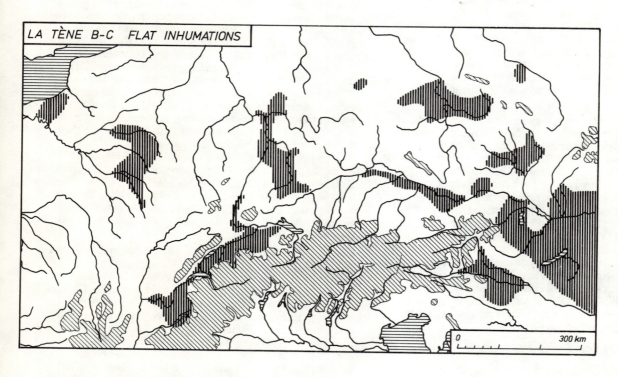

2   *Generalized distribution of flat inhumation burials of La Tène B-C*

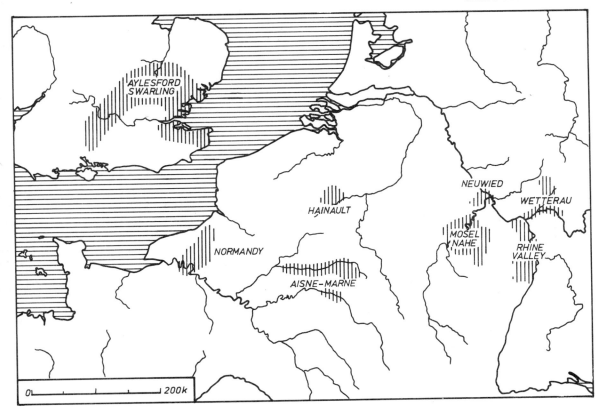

3　Distribution of burials of the North Gallic Culture

imported bronze and silver vessels and other Mediterranean goods, fire dogs and hearth furniture, and much local pottery.

Mention should also be made of the Late La Tène cemeteries of the North European Plain. The hand-made pottery vessels and the metal objects found in the graves of the Germanic cultures are very distinctive and can be readily distinguished, even where the distribution overlaps with that of the North Gallic Culture, as it does in the Wetterau (Schönberger 1952; Uenze 1953; Hachmann, Kossack, and Kuhn 1962). Specific cultures can be identified within the Culture Group, the Przeworsk Culture of Poland, the Oder-Warthe Group, and the Elbe-Germanic Culture. In this last group there is sometimes a division into male and female cemeteries, like the well known male cemetery at Gross Romstedt. The burial rite is almost universally cremation, but unlike the North Gallic Culture both pyre and bones are often deposited into the pit (Brandschüttungsgräber). This group of burials also continues into the Roman Iron Age and is considered elsewhere in this volume by Malcolm Todd (39-43).

In all these burial rite groupings it is most unusual for the cemeteries to be associated with any possible cult or ceremonial centres. Usually each settlement seems to have had its own burial area, and this would account for the small size of many of the cemeteries. Only in the North European Germanic cultures do a number of settlements seem to band together for burial. Exceptions to the rule of the lack of ritual structures are unfortunately those which appear most often in the literature. The henge-like ceremonial or religious centre of the Goloring near Koblenz has a linear barrow cemetery associated which dates from the Urnfield up to Early La Tène, while the

site itself seems to belong to the Hunsrück-Eifel Culture of Hallstatt D/La Tène A (Röder 1948). The only flat inhumation burial of Reinecke B to my knowledge associated with a probable religious structure is the well known site of Libenice (Soudský and Rybová 1962). There is one small group of sites in the Marne, such as Ecury-le-Repos and Fin d'Ecury, but again they are the exception. Of the North Gallic Culture, only Rückweiler has possible ritual timber structures associated. Though it has been recently claimed that a circular building at Frilford (Berks) is ritual because of the presence of a burial inside it (Harding 1972), in fact the converse is probably true. Burial, and especially infant burial, is the hallmark of a domestic site.

Finally it must be remembered that there are many exceptions to the above generalizations—individual sites with their own idiosyncratic burial rites which conform to no pattern. Also we are probably dealing with only the upper classes in the cemeteries, and other irregular and partial burials often turn up on settlement sites such as the hill-forts and minor settlements of the Woodbury Culture and the urban sites of southern Germany and Switzerland. So too there are periods when formal burials are unknown, a blank which in much of Britain and western France covers most of the Iron Age, and during the Late La Tène covers much of central Europe.

The North Gallic Culture

Distribution and sources (Figs. 3, 4)

There is a sporadic scatter of burials along the central Rhine from Strasbourg to Bonn, and also along the Mosel,

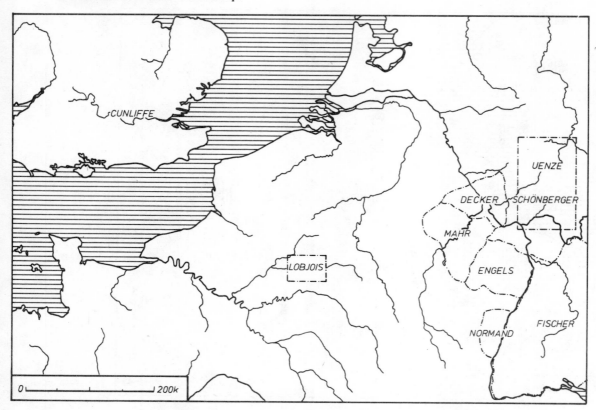

through Luxembourg, southern Belgium, northern France and into south-east England. However there are a number of dense clusters, especially on the Rhine, which form geographically identifiable groups.

The easternmost group runs from the Main around Frankfurt into the plain of the Wetterau, including the salt production centre of Bad Nauheim. It has been well defined by Schönberger (1952) and Uenze (1953). There is a slight overlap with the Germanic type of burial in this area (Hachmann, Kossack, and Kuhn 1962). In the north there is a distinct group in the Neuwied Basin (Decker 1968) and a very dense distribution in the valleys of the Mosel and the Nahe around Trier (Mahr 1967; Haffner 1969, 1971). Further south there are many burials on the western bank of the Rhine, but very few on the eastern bank, and those mainly in the area just north of the Neckar. The Pfalz has recently been studied (Engels 1967), but there are major gaps around Mainz. On the west bank sporadic burials occur as far south as Alsace (Normand 1973) but are virtually absent in Baden-Württemberg (Fischer 1967).

Further west such recent systematic surveys are lacking, other than a brief list produced by Lobjois (1969) for part of the Aisne valley. Otherwise one is forced to rely on old or partial surveys (Hawkes and Dunning 1930; Birchall 1965). The Hainaut group in Belgium has also not been studied in its entirety (Mariën 1961). South-eastern England lacks an adequate corpus, though the evidence in Birchall (1965) and on the Ordnance Survey map (1962) has recently been summarized by Cunliffe (1974, 80).

Characteristics

The predominant burial rite is cremation, though occasional inhumations do occur, as at Owslebury (Collis 1973), St Albans (Stead 1969), Dumpton Gap, Chateau Porcien (Birchall 1965), Filzen, and Schwirzheim (Mahr 1967) and Wallertheim. Isolated burials are known, but more usual are mixed cemeteries with males, females and children all represented. Young infants seem generally to have been inhumed on the settlement, as at Owslebury. Single sex cemeteries such as are found in the Elbe-Western Germanic Group are totally unknown. Only rarely are burials under tumuli, at Lexden, Hurstbourne Tarrant, and Varimpré. However the distribution of the graves in cemeteries with generally no overlapping of graves indicates some form of marker, such as the low mounds noted at Goeblingen-Nospelt (Thill 1966). In England clusters of burials around a rich grave have been noted at Aylesford, Owslebury, and St Albans, and clusters within a cemetery are also recorded at Horath (Mahr 1967). At both St Albans and Owslebury the groups were enclosed within a rectangular ditched area, and continental examples are known in Champagne at Fin d'Ecury and Ecury-le-Repos, and on the Rhône at Wallertheim (Kr. Alzey). However, the majority of the well known ditched enclosures (*Grabgärten*) on the central Rhine belong to the Roman period, even on cemeteries which start in Late La Téne as at Wederath (Haffner 1971), though there is Late La Téne material from the *Grabgärten* at Hambuch (Kr. Cochem) and at Mulheim (Kr. Koblenz) (Mahr 1967).

Some large cemeteries are known—Horath 181 burials, Lebach 200, St Albans 463, and Wederath 1200; the latter two settlements had other cemetery areas in addition. Both were to emerge as towns in the Roman period, and were obviously important centres before the conquest. However there is no evidence of centralization simply for the purposes of burial, and every minor settlement seems to have had its own cemetery. Owslebury seems to have been little more than an extended family group with 20 burials spanning a period of more than 150 years.

The cremated remains were usually collected without pyre material, unlike the *Brandschüttungsgräber* with pyre remains and cremated bone all swept into the pit together, as commonly occurred in the 'Germanic' areas. In some cemeteries the bones are merely scattered into the grave filling (e.g. Owslebury), while at Welwyn Garden City, Stead (1967) suggested the bones were contained within a canvas bag. Normally, however, a pottery vessel was used, a tall pedestal urn in the western areas or an open bowl in the east. Occasionally other containers were used, such as buckets or a wooden box, but it is difficult to see any significance other than social or regional preference in the choice of container.

Grave-goods

Very few burials are found without pottery vessels at all: the 1958 burials at St Albans form one exception (Frere 1959), and usually there are two or more per grave. For the Nahe area south of Trier, Mahr suggests between 4 and 8 is the norm, while on the Moselle and Saar it is less, about 2-3. At St Albans 2-3 is also the norm, but it is higher at Owslebury, around 4-5, even though many of the burials do not have urns. There is little direct evidence that the pots contained anything, but if the much later burials from Les Martres de Veyre now in Clermont-Ferrand Museum are anything to go by, food offerings such as plums, cherries, hazel nuts, coriander seeds, and cakes were placed on the plates.

Jars, plates, and various bowl forms all occur throughout the area, though apparently there is no regular combination of vessel types such as is sometimes found in Urnfield burials. One peculiar phenomenon noted throughout the area is the presence of broken pots or sherds in the graves, but there is usually no evidence that these pots had been burnt on the pyre. Mahr quotes figures for six well excavated cemeteries, and in five cases between 20% and 40% of the pots in the graves were broken, while in the sixth the figure was as high as 66%. Graves at Owslebury vary considerably. In grave 41 several of the pots were represented only by fragments and only one or two of the pots may have been buried intact.

Other than the pottery, brooches are the most constantly recurring grave-good. In some cases the brooches are fragmentary and have been on the pyre. They occur in male, female, and child graves. The only figures available are those quoted by Mahr for Horath:

No. of brooches	0	1	2	3	
No. of female graves	5	4	2	4	(15 graves)
No. of male graves	3	6	1	1	(11 graves)
No. of child graves	8	5	6	1	(20 graves)

The Nauheim brooch may be specifically associated with female graves, and generally women have more brooches than men, but studies of cremated bones to obtain the sex are still too lacking. Other items of personal ornaments or toiletry include chatelaines, axe-shaped razors (Mariën 1971), glass beads, but rarely bracelets or pins.

The occurrence of weapons in burials shows strong regional variation. In Britain there is a vogue at the beginning of Late La Tène for warrior burials with complete sets of equipment, but later, in the Aylesford-Swarling Culture proper, only four possible graves can be quoted, all in the rich category. Each one contains only a protective weapon (shields at Stanfordbury, and Snailwell, and possibly Welwyn Garden City, and chain mail at Lexden), and its presence is clearly highly symbolic. On the Rhine and Moselle there is a similar vogue at the beginning of Late La Tène for weapon burials such as the well known graves from Horath and Wallertheim, in areas where such burials had been rare earlier, but in contrast to England this vogue continues with as many as 10% of the graves at Horath and Wederath, long after the Roman conquest (van Doorselaer 1975). Swords, usually bent, spears, and shields are most common, but spurs occur in several graves at Goeblingen-Nospelt and a helmet at Trier-Olewig (Schindler 1971).

Rich burials

In the eastern part of the area there is a tradition for exceptionally rich burials starting in Hallstatt D and reaching a climax in the Earliest La Tène, with imported Mediterranean goods, local gold- and bronzework of fine craftsmanship, and the provision of a chariot and other horse gear. In the later phases, in Early and Middle La Tène rich burials are rarer, though that at Waldalgesheim is an obvious exception, and M Alain Duval has recently suggested to me that there is a small number of chariot burials in northern France and Belgium which may also be relatively late and form a link with the Late La Tène burials. At the beginning of Late La Tène rich burials are still few in number, but with the upsurge of trade in the 1st century BC, rich burials again become common throughout the whole area of the North Gallic Culture.

The wealth of these graves manifests itself in a number of ways, and there are certain grave-goods which are entirely confined to this group (listed in Appendix I). The characteristics are:

1 The large size of the grave, which is occasionally covered by a tumulus.
2 The large number of pottery vessels.
3 The presence of imported pottery of Italian origin. Most common are wine amphorae (Peacock 1971), but in the later graves Arretine and samian wares also appear. There are graves at Wederath and one at St Albans which have produced only sherds of amphorae, but these are excluded here.
4 Imported bronze and silver vessels of Italian origin. Werner (1954) has distinguished one group of bronzes, probably from Campania, which appear almost exclusively in Late La Tène contexts in the second half of the 1st century BC, but no later than about 15-10 BC.
5 Local bronze vessels, and especially wooden or organic vessels with bronze sheathing, such as tankards, drinking horns, and large wooden buckets of Aylesford type.
6 Domestic equipment of wrought iron, especially hearth furniture such as cauldron hangers and fire-dogs.
7 Wagons and other horse gear.
8 Weapons. Sometimes, especially in Britain, merely a symbolic shield, but at Goeblingen Nospelt there are complete sets with spear, sword, shield, and spurs.
9 A wealth of other miscellaneous objects, sometimes of a personal nature, such as bracelets, brooches or razors, but occasionally gaming pieces, glass vessels, or ornamental bronzes.
10 Men cremated wearing a bear-skin robe (?), noted at Welwyn Garden City and Heimbach-Weis.

The earliest rich burials are all found on the Moselle and central Rhine. At Hoppstädten there is the cremation of a woman with Nauheim brooches accompanied by 60 complete or fragmentary vessels and the remains of a wagon. The burials under the well known Claudian fort at Hofheim also belong to this period, and one burial produced an axe, a sword, part of a bucket, and a collection

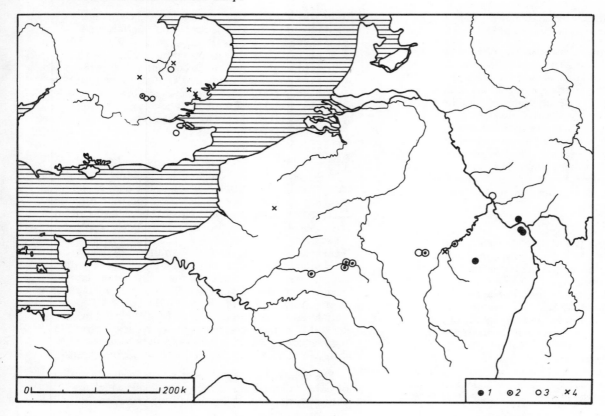

5   *Rich burials of the North Gallic culture: 1. probably pre-Caesarian; 2. c. 50-20 BC; 3. c. 20-10 BC; 4. 10 BC-AD 10 (see Appendix I)*

of burnt horse-gear. Wallertheim (Kr. Alzey) has produced a burial within a rectangular enclosure accompanied by weapons and a number of pottery vessels. A cremation from Armsheim, (also Kr. Alzey) contained a complete wine amphora of form Dressel 1a, the only grave with this early form of amphora outside the Mediterranean coastal area. In the grave there were two local vessels and two bronze brooches of Middle La Tène construction. This short list of burials might be extended by including some of the weapon graves which seem to represent the social class which later was to acquire considerable wealth from the trade with the Mediterranean.

Somewhat later, and probably post-dating the Caesarean conquest of Gaul, are burials with Campanian bronze vessels, Dressel 1b amphorae, and brooches of Colchester construction. The rich burials now extend further west into Britain, with the two graves at Welwyn. In the territory of the Treveri there are the two earliest graves at Goeblingen-Nospelt and what is presumably a rich grave at Trier-Olewig with a Dressel 1b amphora. Doubtless some of the French graves such as Presles-St-Audebert and the three near Rethel belong to this phase. A third horizon is marked by romanized pottery forms which preceded the Gallo-Belgic pottery industry which starts in the last decade before Christ. The Campanian bronze vessels and Dressel 1b amphorae still continue in use. It is typified by the two very rich burials at Goeblingen-Nospelt and Welwyn Garden City, both of which contain pottery of romanized but not true Gallo-Belgic type. Probably the bucket burials at Baldock and Aylesford belong here. Finally there is a late fully Gallo-Belgic phase apparently confined to England and western France belonging to the 1st century AD, ending with the Claudian burials at Stanfordbury. In this last group falls what was probably the richest of all the rich burials, the tumulus burial of Lexden near Colchester.

One feature of these rich graves is their tendency to appear in pairs or in groups, at Welwyn, Stanfordbury, and Goeblingen-Nospelt, or on adjacent sites, around Alzey, Rethel, and Welwyn. Generally these rich burials are not associated with the oppida and other major settlements, Lexden (Colchester) and, outside our area, Kelheim being the exceptions. Unfortunately we know little of the settlements to which the rich burials belonged, but generally they seem to be small, of the size of farms or small hamlets. In south-eastern England they are all within a radius of about 70-80 km from Colchester, along with a series of less rich burials which produce items such as shale vessels, bronze mirrors, and silver brooches (e.g. Great Chesterford). The 70-80 km radius is precisely the zone where the use of gold coinage from Colchester is most concentrated, and the coins and the imports suggest the minor settlements had direct contact with Colchester rather than through intermediary centres such as St Albans.

Chronology

A discussion of the dating must inevitably rely on the typology of brooches, as the only other common grave-good, pottery, is both localized in character and less susceptible to typological study. In terms of typology the earliest brooch types to be found in the North Gallic graves are of Middle La Tène construction with a residual boss on the foot. The type is doubtless broadly contemporary with the Mötschwil or Moravian type which belongs to the final phase at Münsingen and other flat inhumation cemeteries (Hodson 1968; Cizmář 1970). The use of this brooch continues into Late La Tène and it is occasionally found associated with Nauheim brooches (see Appendix II). It is confined to graves on the central Rhine and the Mosel (Fig. 6).

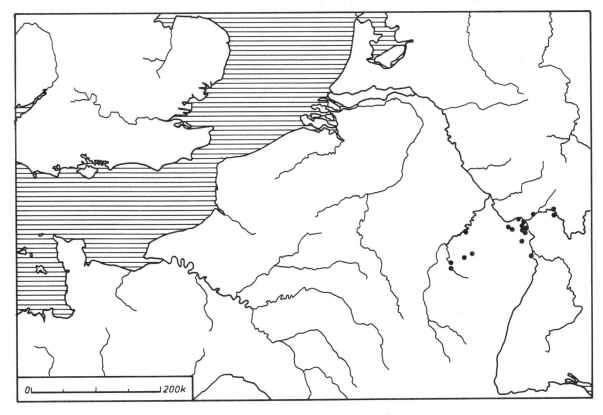

6   *North Gallic burials with Middle La Tène brooches with residual boss (see Appendix IIa)*

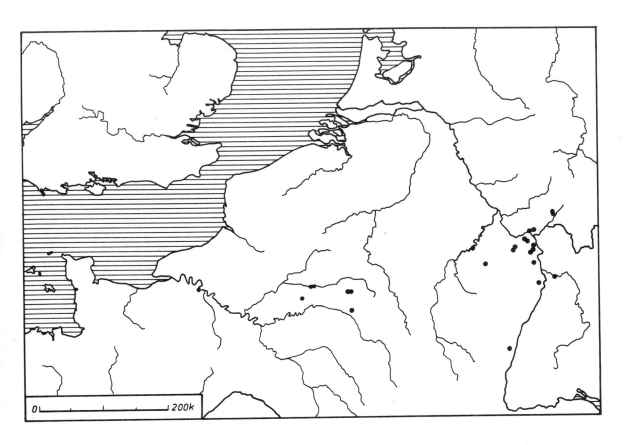

7   *North Gallic burials with plain Middle La Tène brooches (see Appendix IIb)*

BURIAL TRENDS IN THE NEUWIED BASIN	CREMATION				INHUMATION			
		GRAVE GOODS				GRAVE GOODS		
	TOTAL GRAVES	POTTERY ONLY	POTTERY+METAL	METAL ONLY	TOTAL GRAVES	POTTERY ONLY	POTTERY+METAL	METAL ONLY
HA C LAUFELD	262	243	17	0	14	2	8	1
HA D HUNSRÜCK EIFEL I	19	11	7	1	218	38	60	120
LT A IIA	29	16	9	4	161	47	78	24
LT B-C IIB	11	10	1	0	23	3	9	11
LT C-D NORTH GALLIC I	33	9	24	0	1	0	1	0

8   *Burial trends in the Neuwied basin, derived from Joachim 1968*

Next should come the brooches of true Middle La Tène construction with external cord but a plain foot, including such types as Kostrewski A and B. How much these brooches represent an early phase predating Late La Tène is a matter of debate (Bantelmann 1972), but though individual brooches may be late the majority of graves producing them must fall early in the relative sequence. The brooches are again concentrated on the Rhine and Mosel, but are also found in Aisne-Marne group and even in Normandy (Fig. 7).

Brooches of simple Late La Tène construction are found throughout the area including the Aylesford-Swarling Group, for both the type sites have produced examples of the Stradonice/Ornavasso type, which is broadly contemporary with the Nauheim fibula more common in the other groups. But generally the early phase of the Aylesford-Swarling Group is poorly defined, as of the recently excavated cemeteries only Owslebury has produced a good early phase predating the appearance of the Gallo-Belgic pottery. But here the metal finds from the earliest grave are purely of Late La Tène type, though brooches are absent.

Later brooch types are also very widespread, and occur in all the main groups. They are those of Colchester construction such as the Colchester, Langton Down, Rosette, and Shield Bow types, but they continue well into the 1st century AD, when virtually all the area was under Roman control. An important chronological divide is provided by the appearance of Gallo-Belgic pottery from about 10 BC, and it is absent only from the Wetterau Group, which may have disappeared by this time.

The total pattern which emerges from the brooches is of an origin for the burial rite on the central Rhine at the end of Reinecke C, followed by a gradual spread to the west, reaching Britain in Late La Tène. However, it could be argued that we are merely looking at the spread of the idea of including brooches in the cremation burials, or that the early brooch types have a limited distribution and would not be expected in more westerly graves anyway. Until we have some adequate excavations and surveys in northern France to counterbalance the excellent German corpuses, these are questions which cannot be answered.

To consider the origin of a burial rite is perhaps beyond the ability of a prehistorian—who would have guessed the Indian and Neo-Druidic influence which led to the adoption of cremation within our own society? So before one accepts the 'Germanic' influence which is so often postulated to explain the North Gallic Culture, it is advisable to remember there was a general trend towards cremation throughout the La Tène Culture area, and the Late La Tène cremations may merely represent the climax in this development.

The complexity of the development of the burial rite may be demonstrated by the figures for the Neuwied basin derived from Joachim (1968), listed on Fig. 8. The various trends that took place can be summarized as follows:

Cremation	⟶	Inhumation	⟶	Cremation
Pottery goods	→	Metal goods	→	Pottery goods
Tumulus	→	Tumulus	→	Flat cemeteries

In none of the periods was the change absolute, and all the elements of the Late La Tène burials can be found in individual graves in preceding periods. But the situation is further complicated by the fact that Hunsrück-Eifel IIb should be a long period, and is poorly represented in numerical terms, so we perhaps do not know the normal burial rite for the phase immediately preceding the North Gallic Culture.

In summary we can state that the North Gallic burials appeared at the end of Middle La Tène, perhaps between 150 and 100 BC. The earliest dateable graves are all in the eastern part of the area, and the burial rite seems to have spread westwards during Late La Tène.

Other burial rites (Fig. 9)

Outside the North Gallic burial area, pre-Roman burials are notable by their absence. In the zone of the great oppida of southern Germany, there is only one possible cremation at Manching and a couple at Kelheim, which produced the imported 'Kelheim' bronze jug, a shield, a sword, and a fine graphite-ware vessel. However, scattered human bones and fragmentary skeletons are not uncommon in rubbish pits on the settlements, at Altenburg-Rheinau, Breisach-Hochstetten, and Marthalen, and in large quantities at Basel-Gasfabrik and at Manching (Wiedmer 1963). For instance, one pit at Basel produced the skeleton of a woman, wearing a bronze bracelet, and fragments of six other individuals. Similar partial burials are known in Britain in the Woodbury Culture, as at the hill-fort of Danebury, where deliberate exposure and cannibalism have both been suggested (Cunliffe 1974, 292).

The Gasfabrik site at Basel also had a cemetery north of the settlement where some 80 inhumations have been excavated. Most were aligned east-west, extended on their backs, but generally there was little concern to lay the corpse out carefully. It was often difficult for the excavators to be sure to which grave objects belonged, as graves often intersected, and only about 40% had any grave-goods, such as the occasional brooch, wheel-pendant, glass bracelet, or pot. The carelessness of burial reflects that noted in the final stages of the cemetery at Münsingen. Berne, too, has produced a small number of burials, but generally cremations, on the periphery of the oppidum on the Engehalbinsel. The best documented was contemporary with the construction of the ramparts, and contained fragmentary Nauheim brooches and several painted vessels (Müller Beck and Ettlinger 1963).

In central France regular burials occur within the settlements themselves. At Mont Beuvray and Luzech cremations were inserted into the disused ramparts, and at the former were also found within the houses. Both these sites were mainly occupied after the Roman

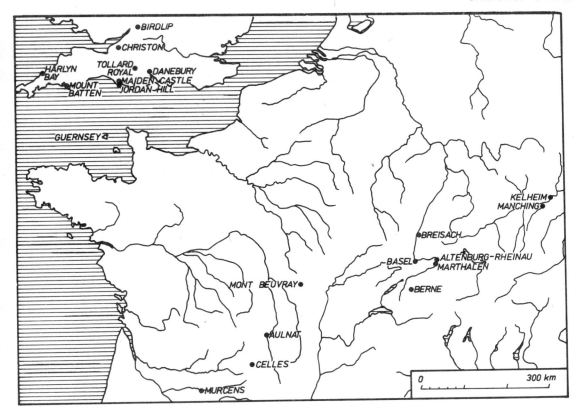

9   *Sites, mentioned in the text, with other burial rites*

conquest. The pre-conquest settlement at Aulnat near Clermont Ferrand has also produced several burials within the settlement (Perrot and Périchon 1968, 1969; Collis 1975a). The adult rite is normally extended inhumation with three or four pots at the head, and the occasional bead, brooch, or knife. But cremation was also practised, especially for children. One child burial consisted merely of a skull accompanied by three or four pots. At Celles (Corrèze) occurred a most exceptional burial under a tumulus, with grave-goods including painted pottery and a large collection of carpenter's tools (Déchelette 1914).

The burial rite on the lower Rhine north of the North Gallic Culture was cremation, as it had been throughout the Iron Age (De Laet 1958). The pottery types, generally hand-made, contrast with those of the North Gallic group, and other grave-goods are rare. Rich burials are totally absent, and we are clearly dealing with a different tradition and rite.

The Channel Islands have produced a comparatively large number of burials (Kendrick 1928). Some, notably those at The Nunnery and Longy Common, both on Alderney, are probably Early La Tène, but the majority of those listed on Guernsey are certainly Late La Tène. The normal burial seems to be extended inhumation in a cist, often unaccompanied, but there are a number of weapon burials closely comparable with those in southern England. The best documented is that from Catioroc illustrated by Kendrick (1928, 190-3) with a sword, shield boss, two spears, a knife, iron and bronze rings, and a wheel-turned pot. Another produced an iron spearhead; a third a pot and sickle; a fourth cist was empty. La-Houge-au-Comte (Câtel), also on Guernsey, contained

a richer burial with two swords, a spear, rings, a bronze vessel, and beads, and a second burial had three pots. Les Issues (St Saviour), Les Adams (St Peter in the Wood), and Lichou Island (also St Peter in the Wood), are other likely Late La Tène burials with weapons on Guernsey, but that from Richmond (St Saviour) may well be earlier. Surprisingly there are no comparable burials on the adjacent mainland of France. Late Iron Age/Early Roman burials are known, especially in south-west Britanny, where they are interleaved with sand-dune deposits, but grave-goods are rare (Giot 1960).

Within Britain other burial rites occur on the northern and western fringes of the Aylesford-Swarling area, generally crouched inhumation. In the Durotrigian territories of Dorset and Somerset several cemeteries are known, at Jordan Hill, Whitcombe, Christon, and Maiden Castle. Compared with the Aylesford-Swarling Group, grave-goods are rare; there are never more than one or two pottery vessels, and brooches are virtually unknown. Three warrior burials are known, at St Lawrence (Isle of Wight) and Whitcombe, and the unusual cremation at Ham Hill (Collis 1973). Both Ham Hill and Whitcombe also produced craftsmen's tools, such as a hammer and an adze. Tollard Royal had a shale bracelet (Wainwright 1968) and Maiden Castle an iron razor (published as an 'axe' [Wheeler 1943, fig. 92:8]), but these are rare items. Further west there are cist cemeteries at Harlyn Bay and Mount Batten, where one burial produced an engraved mirror, but grave-goods are even rarer than in Dorset. Totally exceptional are the rich extended inhumation burials at Birdlip (Glos.), one of which produced the famous mirror, a knife, a bronze bowl, and a brooch datable to the first half of the 1st century AD.

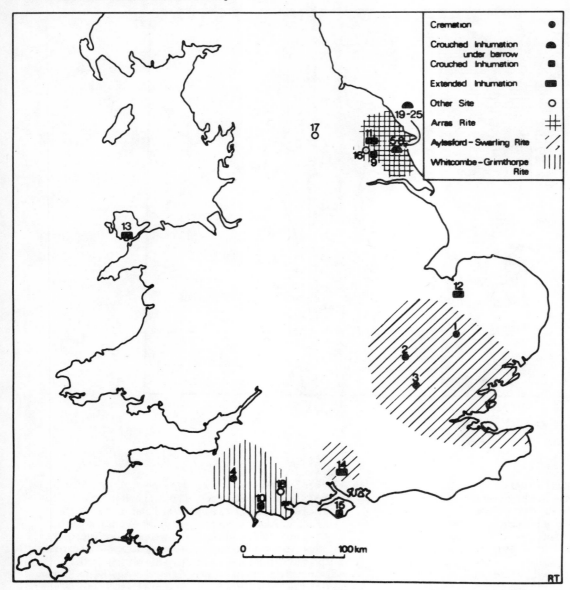

10   *Distribution of burials with weapons in Iron Age Britain (see Appendix III)*

In Yorkshire the Arras group of crouched inhumations under barrows may have continued into Late La Tène, but there is no definite proof. Certainly late in date are the crouched inhumations at Grimthorpe, again generally without grave-goods, excepting the well known warrior burial. There is another definite warrior burial in Yorkshire, the extended inhumation at North Grimston, and similar burials are also known at Shouldham (Norfolk) and Gelliniog Wen (Anglesey) (Collis 1973).

The impact of the Roman conquest

The North Gallic Culture spans the period either side of the Roman conquest, and it is impossible to differentiate between burials belonging to the decade or two before and after 50 BC. It is not until about 30-20 BC or a little later that one can observe a shift in the types of pottery vessels which accompany the burials, with the addition of one or

two new forms such as the handled flagon, and a change in emphasis from bowls towards platters. But this represents a change in culinary and dining habits, and one which occurs on the settlements as well. In other words, the sort of vessels which are being placed in the burials reflect the same functions as before, and there is no essential change in the burial rite. The Aylesford-Swarling Group, at this period still outside the Roman Empire, goes through a similar transformation with the appearance of the Gallo-Belgic pottery industry around 10 BC-AD 10. In the metalwork as well there is no notable difference, with brooches, razors, and other toilet instruments and occasional weapons providing the bulk of finds. If there is any change in rite it is merely a slight shift in emphasis and will only be detected with the detailed analysis of large cemeteries such as Wederath. The burial of weapons was to continue late into the Roman period, and van Doorslaer (1965, 1967) would see this as one sign of native continuity.

In its archaeological manifestation the burial rite of the North Gallic Culture closely resembles that employed by the Roman conquerors, and burials from Roman forts on the Rhine are often indistinguishable from those of the natives. It is in areas where the rite was substantially different that the impact of Rome may be more easy to detect. For instance, burial within a major settlement as is found in central France is in direct contradiction of the Roman edict *'hominem mortuum in urbe nec urito nec sepelito'*. At Mont Beuvray the natives continued their old habits for at least a generation or two, but evidence for what happened at Mont Beuvray's Roman successor *Augustodunum* (Autun) is not available. No-one has yet documented the appearance of Roman burials in areas where burials had not previously existed, but I have gained the impresssion that it was not until the reigns of Augustus or Tiberius at the earliest that the spread takes place into areas such as southern Germany or western France.

Summary

Over most of the area surveyed there was no regular mode of burial, at least one detectable by archaeology, in the half century or more before the Roman conquest. The exception is the area of cremation burials which extends from the central Rhine to eastern England, and which I have termed the 'North Gallic Culture'. Here the burial rite remained essentially the same after the Roman conquest, but elsewhere at least a couple of generations seem to have elapsed before Roman types of burial appeared.

Bibliography

Bantelmann, N (1972) 'Fibeln von Mittellatèneschema im Rhein-Main-Mosel-Gebiet' *Germania* **50**, 98-110

Birchall, A (1965) 'The Aylesford-Swarling culture: the problem of the Belgae reconsidered' *Proc. Prehist. Soc.* **31**, 241-367

Čizmář, M (1970) 'Zur relativ-chronologischen Stellung des jüngsten Horizontes keltische Gräberfelder in Mähren' *Archeologický Rozhledy* **22**, 569-75

Collis J R (1973) 'Burials with weapons in Iron Age Britain' *Germania* **51**, 121-33

Collis, J R (1975a) 'Excavations at Aulnat, Clermont-Ferrand: a first report, with some notes on the earliest Iron Age towns of France' *Archaeol. J.* **132**, 1-15

Collis, J R (1975b) *Defended sites of the Late La Tène in central and western Europe* Brit. Archaeol. Rep. Suppl. Series **2**

Cunliffe, B W (1974) *Iron Age Communities in Britain* (London: Routledge).

Déchelette, J (1974) *Manuel d'Archéologie Préhistorique, Celtique et Gallo-Romaine. 2: Archéologie Celtique et Protohistorique 3: Second Age du Fer ou Epoque de La Tène* (Paris: Picard)

Decker, K-V (1968) 'Die jüngere Latènezeit im Neuwieder Becken' *Jahrb für Geschichte und Kunst des Mittelrheins*, Beiheft **1**

Decker, K-V, and Scollar, I (1962) 'Iron Age square enclosures in the Rhineland' *Antiquity* **36**, 175-8

De Laet, S J (1958) *The Low Countries* (London: Thames and Hudson)

Driehaus, J (1965) ' "Fürstengräber" und Eisenerze zwischen Mittelrhein, Mosel und Saar' *Germania* **43**, 32-49

Engels, H-J (1967) *Die Hallstatt- und Latènekultur in der Pfalz*

Evans, A J (1890) 'On a Late-Celtic urnfield at Aylesford, Kent' *Archaeologia* **52**, 317-88

Filip, J (1956) *Keltové v Strední Evrope* (Prague)

Filip, J (1960) *Celtic Civilization and its Heritage* (Prague: Academy of Sciences)

Fingerlin, G (1971-72) 'Dangstetten: ein augustisches Legionslager am Hochrhein' *Ber. Röm-Germ Komm* **51-52**, 197-232

Fischer, F (1967) 'Alte und neue Funde der Latène-Periode aus Württemburg' *Fundberichte aus Schwaben* NF **18-1**, 61-106

Frere, S S (1959) 'Excavations at Verulamium 1958: fourth interim report' *Antiq. J.* **39**, 1-8

Giot, P R (1960) *Britanny* (London: Thames and Hudson)

Gourvest, J (1956) 'La fibule de Nauheim' *Rhodania*—21e Congrès Vals Aubienus, **2**, No. 1922, 11-13

Hachmann, R, Kossack, G and Kuhn, H (1962) *Völker zwischen Germanen und Kelten*

Haffner, A (1969a) 'Das Treverer Gräberfeld mit Wagenbestattungen von Hoppstädten-Weiersbach, Kr. Birkenfeld' *Trierer Zeitschrift* **32**, 71-127

Haffner, A (1969b) Review of Engels 1967 and Mahr 1967 *Germania* **47**, 229-43

Haffner, A (1971) *Das Keltische-Römische Gräberfeld von Wederath-Belginum* **1**, Graves 1-428

Harding, D W (1972) *The Iron Age in the Upper Thames Basin* (London: OUP)

Hawkes, C F C, and Dunning, G C (1930) 'The Belgae of Gaul and Britain' *Archaeol. J.* **87**, 150-336

Joachim, H E (1968) *Die Hunsrück-Eifel Kultur am Mittelrhein*

Joachim, H E (1973) 'Ein reich ausgestattes Wagengrab der Spätlatènezeit aus Neuwied, Stadtteil Heimbach-Weis' *Bonner Jahrb.* **173**, 1-46

Kendrick, T D (1928) *The Archaeology of the Channel Islands. 1: The Bailiwick of Guernsey* (London)

Kersten, W (1933) 'Der Beginn der La-Tène-Zeit in Nordostbayern' *Praehist. Zeitschrift* **24**, 96-174

Kimmig, W (1938) 'Ein Kriegergrab der Hunsrück-Eifel-Kultur von Horath Kr. Bernkastel' *Marburger Studien:* Festschrift für Gero Merhart, 125-32

Koethe, H, and Kimmig, W (1937) 'Treverergrab aus Wincheringen: ein Beitrag zu Trevererfrage' *Trierer Zeitschrift* **12**, 44-64

Krämer, W (1964) *Das Keltische Gräberfeld von Nebringen, Kr. Böblingen* (Veröffentlichungen der Staatlichen Amtes für Denkmalpflege, Stuttgart)

Laver, P G (1926-27) 'The excavation of a tumulus at Lexden, Colchester' *Archaeologia* **76**, 241-54

Lobjois, G (1969) 'La nécropole de Pernant (Aisne)' *Celticum* **18**, 1-183

Mahr, G (1967) *Die jüngere Latènekultur des Trierer Landes*

Mariën, M E (1961) *La Période de La Tène en Belgique: Le Groupe de la Haine*

Mariën, M E (1971) 'Rasoir romain découvert dans la Grotte de Han (Han-sur-Lesse)' *Helinium* **11**, 213-27

Müller-Beck, H J, and Ettlinger, E (1962-63) 'Die Besiedlung der Engehalbinsen in Bern auf Grund der Kentnissstandes vom Februar des Jahres 1962' *Ber. Röm-Germ. Komm.* **43-44**, 107-53

Normand, B (1973) *L'Age du Fer en Basse Alsace* (Publications de la Société savante d'Alsace et des Régions de l'Est: Collections Recherches et Documents **14**)

Ordnance Survey (1962) *Map of Southern Britain in the Iron Age* (Southampton: Ordnance Survey)

Peacock, D P S (1971) 'Roman amphorae in pre-Roman Britain' in Jesson, M and Hill, D *The Iron Age and its Hill-forts* **161-88** (Southampton: University)

Penninger, E (1973) *Der Dürrnberg bei Hallein*

Perrot, R, and Périchon, R (1969) 'Nouvelles observations sur des vestiges humains de La Tène à Aulnat' *Revue Archéologique du Centre* **32**, 334-58

Röder, J (1948) 'Der Goloring' *Bonner Jahrb.* **148**, 81-132

Rynne, E (1976) 'The La Tène and Roman finds from Lambay, County Durham: a re-assessment. *Proc Roy Ir Acad* **76**, Section C, 231-44

Saldová, V (1955) 'Ploché zarové hrobe halstatska-laténské v ceské mohylové oblasti: Pohřebištĕ v Pzlni-Bílé Hoře a v Rybové Lhote u Sobeslavi' *Pamatky Archaeologický* **46**, 76-100 (German summary)

Schindler, R (1971) 'Ein Kriegergrab mit Bronzehelm der Spätlatènezeit zur Trier-Olewig. Zum Problem des vorrömischen Trier' *Trierer Zeitschrift* **34**, 43-82

Schönberger, H (1952) 'Die Spätlatènezeit in der Wetterau' *Saalburg-Jahrb.* **11**, 21-30

Soudská, E (1968) 'Výzum pozdné halstatského pohrebistĕ v Manetine-Hradku v roče' *Archeologický Rozhledy* **20**, 172-7 (German summary)

Soudský, B, and Rybová, A (1962) *Libenice, Keltská Svatymé ve Stredních Čechách* (French summary)

Stead, I M (1965) *The La Tène Cultures of Eastern Yorkshire*

Stead, I M (1967) 'A La Tène burial at Welwyn Garden City' *Archaeologia* **101**, 1-62

Stead, I M (1969) 'Verulamium 1966-8' *Antiquity* **43**, 45-51

Stead, I M (1971) 'The reconstruction of Iron Age buckets from Aylesford and Baldock' *Brit. Mus. Quart.* **35**, 250-82

Stümpel, B (1961) 'Spätlatènezeitliche Brandgräber aus Ülvershein, Ldkr. Mainz, und Armsheim, Kr. Alzey' *Germania* **39**, 189-96

Thill, G (1966-67) 'Goeblingen-Nospelt' *Hemecht* **18**, 482-91; **19**, 87-98, 149-213

Thill, G (1969) 'Fibeln vom Titelberg aus den Bestandes des Luxemburger Museums' *Trierer Zeitschrift* **32**, 133-71

Uenze, O (1953) *Vorgeschichte der Hessensenke in 15 Karten*

van Doorselaer, A (1965) 'Le problème des mobiliers funéraires avec armes en Gaul septentrionale à l'époque du Haut-Empire romaine' *Helinium* **5**, 118-35

van Doorselaer, A (1967) *Les Nécropoles d'Epoque Romaine en Gaul Septentrionale* (Dissertationes Archaeologicae Gandenses **10**)

Wainwright, G J (1968) 'The excavation of a Durotrigian farmstead near Tollard Royal in Cranbourne Chase, Southern England' *Proc. Prehist. Soc.* **34**, 102-47

Werner, J (1953) 'Keltisches Pferdegeschirr der Spätlatènezeit'
    Saalburg-Jahrb. **12**, 42-52
Werner, J (1954) 'Die Bronzekanne von Kelheim' *Bayerische
    Vorgeschichtsblätter* **20**, 43-73
Werner, J (1955) 'Die Nauheimer Fibel' *Jahrb Röm-Germ Zentralmus
    Mainz* **2**, 170-95
Wheeler, R E M (1943) *Maiden Castle, Dorset* (London: Soc. of
    Antiquaries, Res. Rep. **12**)
Wiedmer, H R (1963) 'Menschliche Skelettreste aus Spätlatène-
    Siedlungen in Alpenvorland' *Germania* **41**, 269-317

Appendix I Rich burials

Unless otherwise stated, information on these burials is
summarized in Stead (1967). The sites are listed in order
from east to west (Fig. 5).

a   Probably pre-Caesarian

1 Hofheim (Werner 1953)
2 Wallertheim (Kr. Alzey), grave 3 (Hachmann,
   Kossack, and Kuhn 1962, taf. 3, 4)
3 Armsheim (Kr. Alzey) (Stümpel 1961)
4 Hoppstädten (Kr. Birkenfeld) (Haffner 1969a)

b   c. 50-25 BC

1 Trier-Olewig (Schindler 1971)
2 Goeblingen-Nospelt C and D (Luxembourg)
   (Thill 1966-7)
3 St Germainmont, Rethel (Ardennes) (Birchall
   1965, fig. 44)
4 Hannogne, Rethel (Ardennes) (Birchall 1965)
5 Chateau-Porcien, Rethel (Ardennes) (Birchall
   1965)
6 Presles-St-Audebert (Aisne) (Birchall 1965,
   fig. 29)
7 Welwyn A and B (Herts)

c   c. 25-10 BC

1 Heimbach-Weis, Neuwied (Joachim 1973)
2 Goeblingen-Nospelt A and B (Luxembourg)
   (Thill 1966-7)
3 Aylesford (Kent) (Evans 1890; Stead 1971)
4 Hertford Heath (Herts)
5 Baldock (Herts) (Stead 1971)
6 Welwyn Garden City (Herts)

d   10 BC—AD 50

1 Wincheringen (Kr. Saarburg) (Koethe and
   Kimmig 1937)
2 Arras 1-4
3 Mount Bures (Essex)
4 Lexden, Colchester (Essex) (Laver 1926-7)
5 Snailwell (Cambs)
6 Stanfordbury A and B (Beds)

Appendix II Brooches of Middle La Tène construction

Unless otherwise stated, the information in these lists is
derived from Bantelmann 1971. All sites are listed from
east to west. Those marked with an * are associated with
a Nauheim brooch.

a   Brooches with a small boss on the foot (Fig. 6)

1 Steinheim
2 Bruchköbel
3 Frankfurt-Fechenheim
4 *Ludwigshafen—Oggerheim

5 Nierstein
6 *Bretzenheim
7 *Uelvesheim
8 Nieder-Olm
9 Hahnheim
10 Heidensheim
11 Ilbesheim
12 Wallertheim
13 Bad Kreuznach
14 Rückweiler
15 Horath
16 Bosen
17 Saarlouis-Roden
18 Beckingen

b   Plain brooches with external cord (Fig. 7)

1 Friedberg
2 *Bad Nauheim
3 Heidelberg
4 Dudenhofen
5 *Nierstein
6 Wallau
7 Heppenheim a.d.W.
8 Ulvesheim
9 Wiesbaden
10 Gau-Odernheim
11 Essenheim
12 Wallertheim
13 Armsheim (Stümpel 1961)
14 Wollstein
15 Hoenheim (Basse Alsace) (Normand 1973)
16 *Rückweiler
17 *Horath
18 St Rémy-sur-Bussy (Marne) (Hawkes and Dunning
    1930, fig. 11, no. 2)
19 La Poterie, Hauviné (Ardennes) (Birchall 1965,
    fig. 43)
20 La-Ford-de-St-Hilaire, Hauviné (Ardennes)
    (Birchall 1965, 322)
21 Chassemy (Aisne) (Birchall 1965, fig. 30, no. 251)
22 Presles-St-Audebert (Aisne) (Birchall 1965,
    fig. 32)
23 Armentières (Aisne) (Birchall 1965, fig. 33)
24 Caudebec-lès-Elbeuf (Eure) (Hawkes and
    Dunning 1930, fig. 11, no. 6)

Appendix III Burials with weapons in Iron Age Britain

For details and bibliography of Nos. 1-18 see Collis 1973.

1	Snailwell (Cambs)
2	Stanfordbury (Beds)
3	Welwyn Garden City (Herts)
4	Ham Hill (Som)
5-8	Eastburn (Yorks)
9	Grimthorpe (Yorks)
10	Whitcombe (Dorset)
11	North Grimstone (Yorks)
12	Shouldham (Norfolk)
13	Gelliniog Wen (Anglesey)
14	Owslebury (Hants)
15	St Lawrence (IoW)
16	Bugthorpe (Yorks)
17	Clotherholme (Yorks)
18	Spettisbury (Dorset)
19-25	Burton Fleming (Yorks) (Information from Dr I M Stead)

Season	Burial No.	Sword	Spearhead	Other Finds
1970	FG.28	—	FG.DT	Knife
1971	FB.10	FB.AQ	—	—
1973	FN.14	FN.BP	FN.CE	Pig bones
1973	FN.17	FN.BR	FN.BS	Pig bones
1974	FA.4	FA.AN	—	—
1974	FA.29	FA.BZ	FA.CA	Pig bones/bone pin
1974	FA.31	FA.CC	FA.CD	—

Addendum

26   Lambay Island, Co Dublin (Rynne 1976)

Burial in Italy up to Augustus

Glenys Davies

Cremation and inhumation would appear to be very different rites: hence they have been used as a convenient criterion for differentiating one group of people from another, especially in the study of Italian prehistory. Thus Randall MacIver wrote in 1927 that

"by the tenth century before Christ, when the new migrations of the Iron Age from the same transalpine countries were complete, the geographical limits of the two burial rites can be sharply defined."[1]

He defined the inhuming area as Italy south of a line running approximately from Rimini to Rome, although he pointed out that cremation north of the line, and inhumation south of it, were not strictly invariable, even at an early date. The explanation seemed simple—invaders from north of the Alps carried the rite of cremation down as far as the Rome-Rimini line, whereas in the rest of Italy inhumation, the rite of the pre-Iron Age inhabitants, continued, generally in trench graves, but with regional variations. More recent research, however, has shown that the situation was not as simple as this, and has challenged the concept of invaders from the north.[2] Nevertheless, the Rome-Rimini line remains a broad division between the areas where cremation and inhumation were the predominant rites during the early Iron Age. Subsequently the situation became more complicated, not so much in the south, where inhumation remained the major rite until Roman influence was sufficiently strong to introduce cremation, but rather in the northern areas, especially Etruria and Rome. Here, after an initial cremating phase, cremation and inhumation alternated and existed side by side, the one emerging above the other in different places at different times. This diversity of burial rite, as well as growing wealth and sophistication, produced a greater variety of tomb types, and an elaborate funerary art, while increasing respect for the individual led to the development of inscribed grave markers for each person, or some other permanent and personal memorial, if only a name over a columbarium niche.

The burial customs of Picenum, the most northerly of the 'inhuming areas', are seen at their most typical in the two cemeteries of Novilara near Pesaro, which cover the period c. 800-650 BC. There the bodies were laid in trench graves roughly plastered on the inside and with a layer of gravel in the bottom (possibly for drainage). The bodies were clothed and placed in a contracted position. Men's graves were well supplied with weapons: in the Servici cemetery only four out of the 37 male burials had no spear at all, many had more than one spear, and some had other arms as well. Some graves were marked with stelae, two of which were decorated with scenes— a naval battle and spiral pattern on one, a hunt and fight scene and inscription on the other. The cemetery at Belmonte is somewhat later (from c. 650 to c. 400 BC), but has similar features, simple earth graves with the bodies laid in a contracted position, with an abundance of arms and some chariots. Remains of chariots have also been found in two 4th century graves in a cemetery at Grottazzolina. The same characteristics are found in other cemeteries ranging in date from the 10th to the 4th centuries, except that on a few sites the bodies were not placed in a contracted but in a supine position. At Terni in Umbria cremations and inhumations have been found belonging to the earliest period (11th century to c. 800 BC), but in the 8th to 4th centuries it seems that only inhumation was practised. The early use of cremation has been attributed to the presence of Villanovans, or pre-Villanovan urnfielders, in this town close to the Villanovan area of Etruria. Early cremation tombs have also been found in Picenum, notably the cemetery of 120 cremation graves of the 8th century found north of Fermo in 1956. The inhumations at Terni are in trench graves covered by low cairns sometimes surrounded by a circle of stones.

Although Greek art came to Picenum via Apulia, Greek influence does not seem to have affected burial customs there. On the other hand, Sennonian Gauls settled between Rimini and Ancona in the 4th century BC, and there are Gaulish graves at Montefortino and Sarsina. These were inhumations in stone-lined trenches covered with earth and each marked with a stone.

To the south of Picenum were the Samnites, a poor and hardy race with burial customs to match. These are illustrated by the necropolis at Aufidena where the same inhumation rite was practised for centuries. The graves are trenches which are generally lined, in the earlier period (7th to 5th centuries BC) with wooden planks, later with stones, and in the 4th century onwards with tiles, and the burials were covered with flat stones or tiles. At the bottom of many graves, as at Picenum, was gravel, on which the body was laid outstretched, dressed and with jewellery or military equipment, the legs sometimes crossed, one hand on the breast, and the head sometimes propped up. These graves were dug in the poorest soil, of which only the minimum was used, some being so narrow that the body had to be turned on its side, some so short that the accompanying spears had to be broken. They were often surrounded by rings of stones or slabs set on end, and men's graves appear to have been marked by a spear, women's by a spindle.

Although this simple formula was adhered to in Samnium itself, Samnites outside their homeland, in Campania, built more elaborate tombs, and sometimes adopted the custom of using an inscribed stone to mark the graves. No such marker has ever been found in the heart of Samnium, and it was only on the more sophisticated sites that imported material was found in graves. In the Paelignian area around Lake Fucino, to the north of Samnium and east of Latium, miniature chamber tombs with a bench for the body were sometimes used, as well as the lined trenches.

In Apulia, the least well documented area of southern Italy, a few of the Bronze Age gallery tombs at Bisceglie near Bari in which collective burial was practised may have continued in use into the Iron Age, but on the whole collective burial was abandoned. In the 8th and 7th centuries, especially in the Peucetian area, *specchie* were used. These are cairns of varying sizes, with a cist made of stone slabs in the centre containing a single skeleton in a contracted position. The normal tomb of the 6th century onwards, when Greek influence was strong, was a trench grave, either containing a coffin made up of slabs of stone or, more rarely, a stone sarcophagus. The body was again placed in a contracted position, which is usual in this area. In the Canusium area there are richer tombs of the 4th and 3rd centuries, the period of prosperity there. These are chamber tombs, often very elaborate, which imitate houses with many painted and stuccoed chambers furnished with tables and beds.

Calabria is represented by two groups of cemeteries, at Torre Galli and Canale. At Torre Galli the 9th to 6th century graves are shallow oblong trenches in which the body was laid fully extended on a bed of twigs and herbs. Usually the sides were reinforced by one or two rows of natural boulders or ill-baked bricks, but the body was not protected from above, and the grave was filled with the material taken out of it. There is no evidence of tumuli or markers. At Canale there is a small group of *fossa* graves, but most people were buried in chambers hewn out of the sides of the sandstone cliffs. These had a square forecourt which narrowed into a passage leading to a burial chamber whose entrance was blocked by a rough monolithic door. The burial chamber was surrounded by a low broad ledge, but the bodies were generally laid in the hollow in the centre of the floor, with only their heads resting on the bench. Such chambers were used as family vaults, but probably for only two generations (that is, parents and their children), since the majority held only two to four bodies. Parallels have been drawn between these rock-cut tombs and those of the Sikels in Sicily. In Lucania, cemeteries near Potenza and Cosenza show that the usual burial rite in the 7th century onwards was inhumation in *fosse* in a contracted position, sometimes in a chest or coffin and covered with stones or tiles.

The usual type of pre-hellenic grave in Campania is a *fossa*, sometimes lined and covered with stone slabs, in which the body was laid in a supine position, or on its side in a contracted position. There are 42 pre-hellenic burials of the 9th and 8th centuries BC at Cumae which are of this type. However, some early cremation graves of Villanovan type have recently been found at several sites near Salerno, Capua, and Paestum. At the major site,

Pontecagnano, the 330 graves represent a mixture of inhumations and cremations of the mid 9th century to about 550 BC; the cremations, which were in biconical ossuaries, predominate in the earlier period, inhumations in the later.

Of the Greek towns in southern Italy, the burial habits of Cumae are probably the best documented. Apart from the pre-hellenic trench graves there are later Greek, Samnite, and Roman burials. There are 68 burials of the Greek period; they are mostly inhumations, the majority in monolithic sarcophagi, or coffins made of slabs of stone which were sometimes covered with tiles, but the body could be merely laid in the earth and there are one or two cremations placed in pottery vessels. Stone-slab coffins continued to be used in the tombs of the Samnite and Roman periods, but some graves were now provided with *loculi* for the grave goods, and small chamber tombs became popular. These contained one or two funerary beds or, more rarely, sarcophagi. Later tombs were covered with stucco and some were painted. Although these were built for inhumations, piles of ashes have been found on the beds in some cases, and there are examples of tombs with a mixture of inhumation and cremation. There is also one tomb which consists of a stele with two niches in the base to hold cinerary urns, which probably belongs to the Roman period. This type of development has parallels elsewhere, although Greek cremations have been found on Ischia and at Sybaris. At Tarentum sarcophagi, robust stone coffins, and chamber tombs were used, in Locri the graves were usually covered in various ingenious ways by tiles, and at Metapontum coffins made of slabs of stone or less commonly of tiles were used.

One conspicuous development in Campania is that of the Samnite painted tomb, parallel to the development in Apulia. Forerunners of the painted tomb can be seen in a 6th century sarcophagus at Tarentum, which has simple painted designs on the inside, and the Tomb of the Diver at Paestum, which resembles a box, with the diver painted on the inside of the lid and a banquet round the sides. The impetus came with the meeting of Samnite with Greek and Etruscan art, resulting in the many painted tombs of Capua, Cumae, Arbella, Allifae, Paestum, and Albanella. The walls are painted with a lower dado and upper cornice, the zone between being decorated with figured scenes divided up by Ionic columns. Favourite themes were chariot races, gladiators, warriors, and sometimes the dead man is depicted, either seated and surmounted by a triangular gable, or sometimes riding towards the world of the dead. One of the earliest of these tombs, the Tomb of the Warrior at Paestum, was probably painted by a Greek artist, although the details are Samnite, but before long the Samnites developed their own style of painting. However, more humble Samnite tombs have also been found in Campania, such as those at Pompeii of the 3rd and 2nd centuries BC, which consist of burials in coffins of stone slabs, or simple trench-graves, some protected by tiles. Only one built tomb has yet been found. This consists of a vestibule and two narrow rooms, in one of which was a skeleton on a bed. At Paestum as well as the richer painted tombs there is a number of Romano-Samnite tile and trench graves.

To return to the northern cremating areas, the northern Villanovans settled in the area around Bologna practised cremation *a pozzo* as the most usual rite. The simplest type of tomb was a cylindrical hole in the earth in which was placed an ossuary, usually a biconical vessel decorated with incised geometrical patterns and covered with an inverted bowl. In more elaborate tombs either the sides of the hole were revetted with small stones, or the ossuary and the accompanying vases were placed in a rectangular cist formed by six stone slabs. The ossuary contained the ashes of the cremated person, amongst which were generally some bones only partially consumed by the fire, and small articles of personal adornment. Weapons and ashes from the pyre were placed on top of the ossuary, cups and bowls around it. These forms of tomb were used in Bologna during the first three periods (from c. 800 to c. 600 BC), the more elaborate forms being more common in the latest phase; the quality of the grave goods improved steadily as time went on. In the fourth or Arnoaldi phase of the 6th century the grave goods are orientalizing but the type of burial remains much the same. Bronze *situlae* could now be used as ossuaries, and sometimes the ossuary and all the grave goods were placed in a large jar or *dolium* which was then buried. Whereas in the earlier periods graves could be marked by rough stones, the Arnoaldi phase sees the first use of sandstone stelae decorated with designs such as sphinxes or heraldic beasts. By the Certosa phase of the 5th century when Etruscan influence was strong in the area, only one-third of the graves are cremations, the rest being inhumations in trench graves. This phase, however, is famous for the Certosa *situla*, which has four zones of repoussé figures of warriors, a funerary procession, animals and rustic scenes. More decoration is also found on the grave stones of this phase: the horseshoe-shaped Felsina stelae are decorated with zones with such themes as sea monsters, the dead riding to the underworld in a chariot, and battle scenes, themes found elsewhere on *situlae* and painted tombs. After c. 400 BC the area, together with much of northern Italy, fell under Gallic influence.

To the east of this area is Venetia, whose main site, Este, has tombs similar to those of Bologna. There is only one tomb which can definitely be assigned to Period 1 (before 950 BC): in this cremated remains were merely buried in the ground. In Period II (c. 950-500 BC) the tomb is generally an oblong receptacle made of six roughly shaped slabs containing a pottery ossuary which is generally conical, but may be biconical. Period III (c. 500-350 BC) sees the flowering of metalwork, especially *situlae*, which were a speciality of the region. The best known of these is the Benvenuti *situla* of c. 500-450 BC, which compares favourably with the Certosa *situla*. Its three zones show scenes of country life, a herd of animals, and warriors. Although such *situlae* were exported to the north, by the 4th century the art had become degenerate and in Period IV (the 3rd and 2nd centuries) Gallic influence was very strong, affecting all but the tomb types, as cremation kept a tenacious hold here. The methods of marking burial plots and graves varied in the different cemeteries in the area.

Burial in Lombardy is represented by the Golasecca culture cemeteries around Lakes Maggiore and Como, where apart from the use of stone circles round the graves the development is similar to that of Bologna and Este. In Period I (900-600 BC) ossuaries were placed in pits lined with pebbles or slabs, in Period II (600-400 BC) in stone cists, and in Period III (400-15 BC), when Gallic influence was strong, inhumation is found alongside cremation. Again, markers vary in the different areas; tumuli, cairns, anthropomorphic stelae, and enclosures are all used. The few examples of burial in Liguria before the Gallo-Roman period are cremations in cists.

From 500 BC onwards, the whole of the northern area was settled by Gauls, of whom the Cenomani, Boii, and Lingones inhumed, usually in trenches lined with stone or brick, but the Insubres cremated. However, by 100 BC, when we see the beginnings of Roman influence, the Gauls had adopted cremation quite commonly, more so in the west than in the east.

Among the southern Villanovans in Etruria, an early development similar to that in early Bologna occurred. Tombs similar to those of Benacci I or Bologna II have been found at Tarquinia and Vetulonia, to Benacci II or Bologna III at Tarquinia, Volterra, Bisenzio, and Vetulonia. Nevertheless, there are variations; the ossuary and grave goods could be placed in another stone container, and although the biconical ossuary covered with a bowl as at Bologna could be used, it was not invariable. Bronze or pottery helmets could be used instead of the bowl, and hut urns, imitating the houses of the living, were sometimes used in Etruria south of Vetulonia and in Latium. In some of the more southern cemeteries, the biconical urn was rare, its place being taken by domestic jars of various shapes, and hut urns.

The next phase, which is early Etruscan rather than Villanovan, differs from its equivalent in the north. At Tarquinia the *pozzo* graves were succeeded by trench graves with the body either laid direct in the ground, or placed in a stone sarcophagus. An early example is the Warrior's Tomb of c. 850-800 BC, while the Bocchoris tomb of c. 730 BC is a transitional form combining features of both trench graves and chamber tombs. Early trench graves are found elsewhere in Etruria, and in 8th century Vetulonia a variant is seen in the construction of a series of circle graves as well as a few trench graves and two or three tumuli. The circles were 15-20 m in diameter, and were made of stone slabs inside which was one or more oblong trench, larger than those of ordinary trench graves. Most were too disturbed for the rite to be ascertained, but cremation may have been more usual in the earlier examples and inhumation in the later.

Seventh century graves are represented at Praeneste, Caere, and in north Etruria, at Chiusi. The very rich Regolini-Galassi tomb at Caere was a tumulus with a central chamber of c. 670 BC and five smaller chambers probably added a generation later. The original chamber was a long gallery divided into two by a slight narrowing forming a chamber and an antechamber. In the antechamber, just before the entrance to the chamber, were two niches; in the right-hand one was a pottery ossuary containing cremated bones. Inside the chamber was an inhumation of a woman—no bed or couch remains, but there may have been a bier. In the antechamber was the skeleton of a warrior on a bronze bed. At Chiusi, the most striking characteristic is the use of cremation in the 7th century, a time when in the rest of Etruria inhumation was beginning to predominate. A new type of ossuary was used, the so-called 'canopic' urn. At first faces were attached to the urn, later a head was modelled on the neck, and then arms and the upper part of the body was added. These urns remained popular for a long time and are found in chamber tombs. Two of the earliest chamber tombs are the Poggio alla Sala (c. 670 BC) and Pania tombs. The Poggio alla Sala tomb was a single chamber excavated from the rock containing a bronze chair on which stood a bronze ossuary containing cremated bones. The Pania tomb, however, was a chamber built of travertine blocks which contained a stone couch on which the skeleton found on the floor presumably once rested. In the corner was a bronze *situla* containing a bronze ossuary inside which were cremated bones. Thus in the 8th and 7th centuries all over Etruria there is a definite mixture of burial types, not only in the same cemetery but even in the same tomb.

In the south of Etruria inhumation remained the major rite; burials both in chamber tombs and in tumuli were usually on rock cut beds or, after c. 300 BC in Tarquinia, Tuscania, and Vulci, in sarcophagi, often with effigies of the dead reclining on the lids. Trench graves also continued to be used in large numbers in many places. Chamber tombs cut into the hillside were used in large numbers in Tarquinia; these were often richly painted inside with pictures of banquets, hunting, and the underworld, but there is only one example of a painting with a mythological subject. Chamber tombs also predominated over tumuli at both Veii and Vulci, where painting was less common. Caere favoured large tumuli built on stone bases, containing one or more groups of burial chambers designed to imitate houses containing funerary beds and chairs hewn from the rock. Outside stood tombstones, cylindrical for men, chest-shaped for women, with inscriptions, probably to identify the individuals buried within. Later, simple underground chambers were built, consisting of single rooms. Painting is rare at Caere. In Orvieto another type of tomb was built, partly above ground, and in the more inland valleys rock tombs were cut into the vertical cliffs forming elaborate façades similar to those of houses. These connected with one another by stairways cut into the face of the cliff. There are two types of these tombs: cubes which stuck out of the cliffs and gabled tombs with façades flush with the cliff. Despite the elaborate pretence outside, inside the tombs were roughly hewn chambers making no attempt to imitate houses. The rite was generally inhumation.

In the north the obstinate continuation of cremation in Chiusi is echoed elsewhere. At Volterra chamber tombs were cut from the rock to serve as family vaults for generations, and large numbers of alabaster or tufa ash containers and vases were placed round the walls and the central column. The well known ash containers, of which there are over 600 in the Volterra museum, are seldom more than 2 ft in length, with a recumbent figure of the dead on the lid, all the attention being paid to the head at the expense of the small body. On the sides are scenes of the descent into the underworld, mythology, and daily life. At Chiusi itself canopic urns continued in use, and in the 4th century a type was developed which consisted of a large seated figure with a detachable head, but a rectangular urn similar to those of Volterra but of tufa or terracotta was also used. Despite the length of time that cremation prevailed at Chiusi, in the 3rd century, as in many other places, inhumation in sarcophagi was practised. At Perugia there are a small number of tombs in which both cremation and inhumation took place, inhumation in stone sarcophagi which were frequently decorated, cremation in bronze vessels and travertine urns; the latter are similar to those at Volterra and Chiusi, and there is a local type which is a small replica of a house. At Populonia, however, chamber tombs and tumuli tended to contain burials in sarcophagi: another type of tomb commonly found there was shaped like a rectangular shrine. Right at the end of the period (c. 100 BC) the tomb of the Volumnii at Perugia illustrates in a developed form the Etruscan conception of the tomb as a house: on the other hand the ornamental style of its ash chests is so hellenized as to belong to another world.

The areas of the Faliscans and Latium are backward in comparison with Etruria. In the *pozzo* tombs of Falerii and Narce the biconical ossuary was not used; there is only one fragmentary example of a hut urn, and instead most of the ossuaries were oval or spherical cooking pots. Another custom peculiar to this area is that of cutting a small cupboard or *loculus* out of the side of the *pozzo* to hold grave goods. Inhumation was adopted at a very early date: *fossa* graves are found alongside *pozzi* in the 9th and 8th centuries, and chamber tombs were favoured in the area, although they were never very imposing. Two more developed types of *fossa* grave were also common: one contained a *loculus* as well as a sarcophagus, the other, halfway between a chamber tomb and an ordinary trench grave, contained *fosse* for more than one corpse. Biconical ossuaries are not found in Latium, but are replaced by hut urns and domestic pots, with or without a *dolium*. Cremations were rapidly replaced by *fossa* graves, in which the body was protected by stones and stone slabs or a wooden coffin. Again, *loculi* were used in trench graves, but chamber tombs were rare, a situation also found in Rome.

So far in this account Rome has been conspicuous by her absence, largely because, until the more elaborate tombs of the 1st century BC, she seems to have been a cultural backwater, at least as far as burial was concerned. Early cemeteries have been found in the Forum between the Sacra Via and the temple of Antoninus and Faustina, and on the Esquiline; a few tombs have also been found on the Quirinal, the Palatine, and the Velia. Among the earliest burials in the Forum[3] there are approximately the same number of cremations *a pozzo* as inhumations *a fossa;* these are mainly burials of adults. However, the later graves are all of children under ten, and are associated with the hut habitation which existed in the area at that time. With only one exception, these later burials are inhumations in hollowed tree-trunk coffins or in jars, or in trenches protected or unprotected by stones. The early graves of the Esquiline are nearly all inhumations; only three cremations have been found. In many cases the construction of the tomb is not known, but the commonest type seems to be a trench revetted with rough tufa stones with a pseudo-vault over the remains. A few burials were in cists made of stone slabs, and there is one chamber tomb of the 6th century. Most of the graves held only one body in a supine position, but in some there may have been both a man and a woman buried in one grave. On the Quirinal there are two *pozzo* cremations and one inhumation in a terracotta sarcophagus which imitated a tree-trunk coffin. The grave on the Velia was of a child buried in a *dolium;* on the Palatine the remains of two child inhumations have been found.

Our knowledge of burial in Rome during the early part of the Republic is derived mainly from the Esquiline cemetery. Here the most common type of tomb was for a long period a simple *fossa* protected by slabs of stone, either forming a gable or a coffin. One monolithic sarcophagus has been found. Chamber tombs were rare; only twelve have been found, of which only one apart from the one already mentioned can be dated before the 4th century. A transitional type of tomb was also used which is larger than a *fossa* and built of blocks of tufa laid in courses to form a false vault, open at the top. The most famous of the chamber tombs is that with a painting showing a figure labelled Q. Fabius talking to another, M. Fannius. This has been variously dated, but the most likely explanation is that the picture shows an episode of the Samnite wars, and that Q. Fabius is the Q. Fabius Maximus Rullianus who was consul five times between 322 and 295 BC.

Although cremation was practised to some extent throughout the time the Esquiline necropolis was in use, inhumation was more common. Ossuaries of Gabine stone have been found, dated by von Duhn to the 4th century, although they may be earlier. Only two contain anything dateable; one belongs to the 4th century, the other, which comes from a chamber tomb, to the 3rd century or later. They are rectangular monolithic chests, in most cases with gabled lids, short legs, and slightly recessed panels, suggesting a crudely formed house; on some architectural details are shown. Some jars containing cremated remains have also been found but there is no evidence that cremation ever predominated in this cemetery.

In the 3rd and 2nd centuries BC the area became infamous for its mass burials of the poor in *puticuli*. These paupers' graves were large trenches into which the bodies were thrown and then left to rot until the trench was filled in. Varro, Festus, Horace (twice), and Porphyrio[4] all comment on the use of the Esquiline for this purpose; 75 trenches believed to be *puticuli* were found by Lanciani in an area north of the Porta Esquilina. They were rectangular pits 4-5 m square, lined with irregular blocks of tufa, containing the remains of burned and unburned bodies together with numerous ordinary vases and lamps. He estimated that there were several hundred of these pits. It is not surprising, then, that in the 1st century BC burial on the Esquiline was being limited, and in certain areas prohibited altogether by magisterial decrees. The necropolis became such a nuisance that in 35 BC it was included in the gardens of Maecenas.

Both Pliny[5] and Cicero[6] named inhumation as the primitive rite in Rome, and implied that this was later superseded by cremation, since Pliny said that many Roman families, especially the Gens Cornelia, retained inhumation as a family rite while others were cremating their dead, and Cicero says that Sulla was the first of the Cornelii to be cremated. It has been assumed on this evidence that the inhumations found in the early 3rd century tomb of the Scipios were at that time unusual in Rome. This, however, is contradicted by the evidence of the Esquiline cemetery, where it seems inhumation was for a long time the more usual rite, although cremation was also practised. This is in keeping with the evidence of the Twelve Tables[7], which assumed the existence of both rites. A possible explanation of the difference between the literary and the archaeological evidence is that the literary evidence refers to the customs of the upper classes, whereas the Esquiline rapidly became notorious as a burial place for the lower classes. However the evidence of Cicero[8] is that even in the late Republic the cemetery was still a fitting place for those of noble ancestry to be buried, and some of the chamber tombs are of this later period.

The tomb of the Scipios is, however, unusual in Rome because of its imposing size and the decorated sarcophagus of Scipio Barbatus. This tomb is 300 m inside the Porta Appia of the Aurelian wall. It is hollowed out of the tufa and decorated with simple architectural elements and paintings, probably of military scenes; it probably dates to the 2nd century BC. The tomb has two entrances, one to the main single gallery which has burial niches on either side, the other to a large chamber which has a gallery on all four sides. The sarcophagi of eight members of the Gens Cornelia were placed in the *loculi*. That of L. Cornelius Scipio Barbatus, consul in 298 BC, is the earliest and that of Paulla Cornelia, wife of Hispalla, who died c. 130 BC, is the latest, except for two burials of the 1st century AD. All the sarcophagi apart from that of Barbatus are plain except for inscriptions: that of Barbatus is an imposing piece decorated with volutes on the top, and below architectural mouldings with metopes containing double rosettes and triglyphs. The inscription was placed both

between the volutes and below the metopes and triglyphs. In 1956 another tomb of the Cornelii was found on the Via Cristoforo Columbo which contained a sarcophagus cover in peperino with the name L. Cornelius, son of Cnaeus, and another lid of limestone with the inscription *P. Cornelio P. F. Scapola / Pontifex max.* which are thought to be earlier, probably dating from the end of the 4th or the beginning of the 3rd century.

These tombs indicate another tendency—to place tombs along the roads leading from the city. This may at first have been done only by the wealthiest, but by the end of the 2nd century was taken up by all classes, as can be seen by a large number of cinerary vases found in a chamber in the Vinea di San Cesario. This is the earliest known instance of a large collection of cremation urns under one roof in Rome; the same effect was later achieved by *columbaria*, where each small building contained hundreds of niches. Marion Blake[9] suggests that the closing of the Esquiline cemetery precipitated the growth of these *columbaria*, but the earliest example, dating probably between 55 and 35 BC was found in the Esquiline cemetery itself. Such structures provided a more dignified type of burial than the *puticuli* for the lower classes, and corporations were organized to build and rent them out niche by niche, so that it was no longer necessary to belong to a wealthy family to have a part share in the tomb. The remains of a few early *columbaria* survive. On the north side of the Via Praenestina, in an area where many *columbaria* have been destroyed, is the columbarium of the freedmen of the Statilii. Three *columbaria* were discovered in the Vigna Codini; the first, which has room for 450 people, has 295 epitaphs of freedmen, slaves, and workmen who died during the reigns of Tiberius and Claudius. The niches of the second were distributed in AD 10, and the third belongs to the early Empire. A fourth surviving *columbarium* of the early empire is that of Pomponius Hylas, which was built under Tiberius; again the niches appear to be owned by people who were not related to one another.

Some individual tombs were built in the late Republic. The tomb of Sulpicius Galba, probably the consul in 108 BC, is a simple rectangular structure of Monte Verde tufa with a travertine block for the inscription, and a pair of fasces carved in the façade on either side of it. The tomb of C. Poplicius Bibulus on the eastern side of the Victor Emmanuel monument was probably built c. 70-60 BC. It is again a simple rectangular building with a travertine façade in the centre of which is a window-like opening, probably intended to hold a statue. Above is a frieze of bucrania, garlands, and paterae, held up by four Doric pilasters, two to each side of the niche. Two framed spaces for inscriptions were placed on the wall, but the inscription was in fact on the podium. The location of the burial itself was not recorded.

Four chamber tombs, the two most easterly of which had a continuous frontage, were found on the Villa Wolkonsky estate near the Via di S. Croce in Gerusalemme. The first tomb, built by a P. Quinctius for himself, his wife, and his freedwoman, had a peperino façade with the inscription and two plain shields cut in low relief. The cella contained four inhumations and four cremations; the original owners appear to have been inhumed. The second tomb, of the freedmen of the *gentes* Clodia, Marcia, and Annia, had two cellae, each with its own doorway. In one were six niches each containing two urns, and in the other fourteen cremations in urns and one inhumation in a *fossa*. On the façade, as well as the inscription, were two inset travertine blocks, one over the entrance to each cella; one had three portrait busts, two male and one female, the other two, one male and one female, carved in relief in arched niches. The other tombs in the row were largely destroyed. A later tomb is that of C. Sulpicius Platorinus, a *triumvir monetalis* in 18 BC; the other inscriptions inside the tomb date from Augustus to the Flavians. The tomb is again rectangular with an acanthus frieze. Statues of Platorinus and his wife stood on either side of the door. Inside were large niches, which contained urns and decorated ash chests; all the burials were cremations.

As well as these comparatively modest late Republican tombs there are also a certain number of very imposing tombs—and the lunatic fringe. To the lunatic fringe I have assigned the Cestius Pyramid, the similar 'Meta Romuli', and the Baker's Tomb of Eurysaces, which is probably made up of stylized corn measures topped by a frieze showing the processes of bread-making. The more imposing tombs are the circular mausolea, of which the mausoleum of Augustus is one. Opinions differ as to their relative dating: Marion Blake[10] places most examples before the mausoleum of Augustus, but Holloway dates most of them after it. There are many examples of the type all over Italy, the main feature being a large circular drum inside which was the burial chamber. One example of these is the tomb on the Via Appia of Caecilia Metella, who was probably the wife of M. Licinius Crassus, quaestor in 54 BC. It has a square podium on which stands a circular drum faced with travertine, and a frieze of marble decorated with bucrania, garlands, and shields. The mausoleum of Augustus itself, built in 28 BC, in the Campus Martius, is the largest of all. Various reconstructions have been suggested, but it is likely that it was 87 m in diameter with five concentric walls, the outermost one retaining the mound, and with the burial chamber, entered by a narrow passage cutting through the ring walls, inside the innermost wall. In the centre was a pillar on which stood the statue of Augustus, which rose above the top of the mound. In the mausoleum were buried many members of the Julio-Claudian house, as well as Vespasian, Nerva, and Julia Domna.

That brings to a conclusion a very brief survey of the various methods of burial in Italy in this period, but I would like to make a few generalized points about the period as a whole. The most obvious features are the great variety of tomb types and the changes in burial custom, not always closely linked to geographical areas or known groups of people. There is also a natural tendency for more elaborate tombs to develop at times of prosperity. It is interesting that the tombs of the Roman Republic seldom reach anything like the same standard of opulence as those of Apulia, Campania, and Etruria. We have only two examples of painted tombs of the Republic in Rome, those of the Fabii and Scipios, and they were built at a time when large painted tombs had been flourishing elsewhere for some time. Subsequent research may change this picture, but at present it seems that Rome's heyday began only in the late Republic.

Secondly, there is the growth of the family vault, or tomb designed to contain more than one body. The early Iron Age in Italy sees the almost universal use of individual graves, whether cremations or inhumations. Forerunners of collective burial can possibly be seen in the habit in some areas of grouping several trenches in a circle, and in those instances where the grave goods appropriate to both men and women have been found in the same grave or two skeletons have been found in the same trench. Although chamber tombs often contained only one burial, many contained a few bodies and were probably intended as a family tomb lasting only a generation or so, but there are also many bigger tombs, as at Volterra, which show a tendency to think on a larger scale. The chamber tombs with provision for only one burial suggest that chamber tombs were not built in order to facilitate collective burial; it may be that costly tombs were used for more than one burial to offset the expense. The *columbarium* is another thing again, belonging to a world where the lower sections of society desired a small family or individual tomb but could not afford one. A corner of a masonry tomb where their remains would be kept safely and visibly no doubt seemed more appropriate than an earth grave.

Thirdly, there is the development of a tomb art. The earlier graves show little evidence of objects even specifically made for the grave, let alone decorated with a specific series of pictures. It is difficult to assess precisely when such a tomb art began, but a series of subjects thought of as appropriate to the tomb may be seen on the bronze *situlae* and tombstones of the north, tomb paintings in Etruria and Campania, and the later decorated ash chests and sarcophagi. In the earlier periods these pictures deal with occupations of life—hunting, fishing, banqueting, and the journey to the Underworld and existence there. It is later than mythological scenes are found, mainly on ash chests and sarcophagi, the result of hellenistic influence. One idea that was particularly popular, especially in Etruria, was that of the tomb as a house, whether the house was an early hut urn or a later ash chest, or a tomb imitating a house either inside of outside.

A fourth development is towards the use of individual and personal grave markers or monuments. Many early trench tombs may have had markers of some sort, if only the mounds caused by filling them in, because the graves do not impinge on one another. However, the concept of a marker to mark an individual's grave can only be supposed when stelae are inscribed (although the possibility of painted names or perishable markers cannot be ruled out). There is no clear evidence that graves were marked individually in Samnium and Calabria, but in Picenum a small group of graves had stelae, one of which was inscribed. In Apulia rough anthropomorphic stelae were sometimes used, and in Campania there are a variety of types, including those of Capua which were decorated with scenes of the dead and his family. The Samnites, who did not use inscribed stelae in Samnium, used them in other areas. In the north, there are again several types of stelae, including the Felsina stones and those of Este, both commonly inscribed. Outside the chamber tombs at Chiusi were found markers to identify the individuals buried inside, but on the whole in the later period the Etruscan dead were identified by a portrait on the top of the ash chest or sarcophagus, and an inscription on the front. This illustrates another tendency which became important in Rome: the use of funerary portraits; the Villa Wolkonsky tomb with its two sets of portraits in the façade is an early example of this particular custom in Rome. The use of decorated ash chests and grave altars with personal inscriptions and often with a portrait was a common feature of the early Empire.

By the reign of Augustus Roman burial customs were spreading all over Italy. 'Roman burial customs' at this period means the rite of cremation, the burnt remains being placed in a container which was itself put in a *columbarium* or family tomb. Thus the rich variety of Italian burial customs began to conform to Rome's mould. Nevertheless, this did not mean that burial customs were to remain any more static under the Empire than they had done before, since Rome was to revert once again to inhumation in the 2nd century A.D.

Notes

1 MacIver 1927, 1.
2 cf. Hencken 1968, II, ch. 21: 'The Appennine Bronze Age and the Pre-Villanovan Urnfields'; ch. 32: 'Who were the Villanovans and Etruscans?' He replaces the idea of one or two major 'invasions' from the north with that of more numerous and smaller settlements, primarily from the Aegean area. He also suggests that there were separate settlements of Villanovans round Bologna, in Etruria, and in Campania, rather than a movement from one area to another. He summarizes the views of other scholars such as those of Bernabò Brea and Cavalier that urnfield burial was a religious idea which evolved without ethnic change.
3 The date of the earliest burials in the Forum, and indeed which of these graves should be considered the earliest, has been contested. Gjerstad considered the earliest tombs to belong to the 8th century, but others (Müller-Karpe and Peroni) have placed them much earlier, in the 10th or even 11th century (cf. Hencken 1968, App. D).
4 Varro *L. L.* v. 25; Festus 216; Horace *Sat.* 1.8.10; 1.8.14-16; Porphyrio *ad Hor. Epod.* v. 100.
5 Pliny *N. H.* vii. 187.
6 Cicero *de Leg.* II.22.56
7 *Twelve Tables* III.890-3
8 Cicero *Phillipic* IX.17
9 Blake 1947, 62
10 Blake 1947, 67; Holloway 1966

Select Booklist

Early Italy

MacIver, R (1924) *Villanovans and Early Etruscans* (Oxford: Clarendon)
MacIver, R (1927) *The Iron Age in Italy* (Oxford: Clarendon)
MacIver, R (1928) *Italy before the Romans* (Oxford: Clarendon)
Hencken, H (1968) *Tarquinia, Villanovans and Early Etruscans* (Cambridge, Mass: American School of Prehistoric Research, Peabody Museum Bulletin 23)
von Duhn, F and Messerschmidt, F (1923/1939) *Italische Gräberkunde* 1 (1923), 2 (1939) (Heidelberg)
*Pallottino, M, et al (eds) (1974/1975) *Popoli e Civiltà dell'Italia Antica* 2, 3 (1974), 4 (1975)
Gierow, P G (1966/1964) *The Iron Age Culture of Latium* 1 (1966), 2 (1964) (Acta Instituti Romani Regni Sueciae 24)
Bryan, W R (1925) *Italic Hut Urns and Hut Urn Cemeteries* (Papers and Monographs of the American Academy at Rome 4)
Holland, L A (1925) *The Faliscans in Prehistoric Times* (Papers and Monographs of the American Academy at Rome 5)
*Colonna, G (ed) (1976) *Civiltà del Lazio Primitivo* (Catalogue to Rome Exhibition)
*Colonna, G (1974) 'Preistoria e protoistoria di Roma e del Lazio' *Popoli e Civiltà dell'Italia Antica* 2, 275-346
Narce: *Monumenti Antichi* 4, 400-506
Salmon, E T (1967) *Samnium and the Samnites* (Cambridge: CUP)
Aufidena: *Monumenti Antichi* 10 (1901), 225-638
*Ordona (Foggia): 'Scavi nella necropoli' *Not Sc* (1973), 285-399
*Oppido Lucano (Potenza): 'Rapporto preliminare sulla prima campagna di scavo' *ibid* (1972), 488-534

The Greek Cities and Campania

Cumae: *Monumenti Antichi* 22, 448-766
Locri: *Not Sc* (1911), 3-26; *ibid*, suppl to 1912 (1917), 101-67
Tarentum: *ibid* (1940), 426-505
Metapontum: *ibid* (1966), 136-231
Paestum: Napoli, M (1970) *La Tomba de Tuffatore* (Bari)
Campania: 'Republican Capua' *Pap Brit Sch Rome* (1959), 80-131; pt 3 'Campanian stelae'
*d'Agostino, B (1974) 'Il mondo periferico della Magna Graecia' *Popoli e Civiltà dell'Italia Antica* 2, 179-271

Etruria

*Coarelli, F (ed) *Etruscan Cities* (Milan)
Scullard, H H (1967) *The Etruscan Cities and Rome*
Romanelli, P (1951) *Tarquinia—La Necropoli e il Museo* (Rome)
Pallottino, M (1960) *La Necropoli di Cerveteri* (Rome)
Shaw, C (1939) *Etruscan Perugia* (Baltimore)
Ward-Perkins, J B (1961) 'Veii—topography and history' *Pap Brit Sch Rome* 1961, 39-46
*Veio: 'Continuazione degli scavi nella necropoli villanoviana in località Quattro Fontanili' *Not Sc* (1972), 195-384

Rossi, G (1925) 'Sepulchral architecture as illustrated by the rock façades of central Etruria' *J Rom Stud* 15, 1-59
*Volterra: 'Gli scavi degli anni 1960-65 nell'area della necropoli di Badia' *Not Sc* (1972), 52-136

Rome

For individual tombs see:

Platner, S, and Ashby, T (1929) *A Topographical Dictionary of Ancient Rome* (London)
Nash, E (1951) *A Pictorial Dictionary of Ancient Rome* 1 and 2 (London)
Gjerstad, E (1956) *Early Rome* 2, 'The Tombs' (Acta Instituti Romani Regni Sueciae 18)
Esquiline: *Monumenti Antichi* 15 (1905), 43-248
Ryberg, I (1939) *An Archaeological Record of Rome* (London)
Frank, T (1924) *Roman Buildings of the Republic* (Papers and Monographs of the American Academy at Rome 3)
Blake, M E (1947) *Ancient Roman Construction in Italy from the Prehistoric Period to Augustus* (Washington: Carnegie Institute Publication 570)
Villa Wolkonsky tombs: *Not Sc* (1917), 174-9
Cordingly, R A, and Richmond, I A (1927) 'The Mausoleum of Augustus' *Pap Brit Sch Rome* 10, 23-35
Holloway, R R (1966) 'The Tomb of Augustus and the Princes of Troy' *Amer J Archaeol* 171-3
Toynbee, J M C (1971) *Death and Burial in the Roman World* (London: Thames and Hudson)

* The books marked with an asterisk have all been published since this paper was written. The recent work in Lazio is of particular interest, showing as it does that early Latin culture in general, and the tombs in particular, were by no means as poor and insignificant as has hitherto been assumed. This was amply illustrated by the exhibition held in the spring of 1976 at the Palazzo Esposizione in Rome entitled 'Civiltà del Lazio Primitivo'. The catalogue to this exhibition is itself an important contribution to the study of Latin culture. The series *Popoli e Civiltà dell'Italia Antica* is a collection of a number of long articles on various areas of Italy, written by different authors and of varying degrees of relevance to the study of burial.

A quantitative approach to Roman burial

Rick Jones

A question that might have received more consideration at the Conference is why we are worrying about graves at all. A tacit assumption seems to have been made that such research is worthwhile, but perhaps we should consider exactly what we are studying, what is the nature of the evidence, what it can tell us, and what it cannot. Burial practices themselves deserve attention if only because burials provide so large a proportion of our field monuments. This draws us into matters such as the location and organization of cemeteries, their relationships with settlements, and the precise details of the burial rite as it survives. Yet it is also through burials that we come closest to the individuals who lived in the ancient world. Buried bones can tell us something of what they looked like, how big they were, and what diseases they suffered from. The overwhelming importance of burials in these matters is unquestioned. Difficulties arise when we are tempted by our nearness to these individuals to advance our interpretations into problems of belief and social organization. To draw conclusions about the ideas of living from the remains of the dead is fraught with complications. Perhaps following Ucko (1969) we may all appear to be convinced of this. Indeed if we believe our own declarations, we can happily say that we are all sceptics now. It may be, however, that in the Roman period, with the aid of the extra information available from historical sources, we can progress a little further than in prehistory. Ucko tended to assume that the problems of the Roman period were all solved long ago (Ucko 1969, 274). Much of what we know about ideas, certainly from written sources, is concerned with the situation in Rome and Italy and the ruling classes; what was happening across society in the provinces is quite a different matter.

In considering any local variations, it is of little use to look at the few remarkable examples of grand mausolea. If we seek to form any views on such topics as the spread of specifically Roman burial practices, it is essential to examine the mass of graves of the Roman period. To follow Wheeler, quoting Pitt-Rivers, 'common things are of more importance than particular things, because they are more prevalent' (Wheeler, 1956, 30). Yet the scale of the problem is not generally appreciated. It may be freely admitted that the city of the dead had a much greater population than that of the living, but by how many? A medium-sized Roman town might have had a stable population of about 2000 (Duncan-Jones 1974, 259-77). If that size was maintained for only two centuries, with a notional annual crude mortality rate of 25 per thousand, the cemetery population would have been some 10,000. At a city as large as Lyon, where a recent estimate has put the population total somewhere between 50,000 and 80,000 (Audin 1965, 133), the same formula over only two centuries gives between 250,000 and 400,000 burials, and over the whole of its Roman life perhaps twice those figures. In qualification, this is an extreme example and the formula is entirely notional. In the first place, we have very little real idea of the total populations of Roman towns and how they developed after their initial growth. Nevertheless the figure of 2000 does not seem excessive. The mortality rate is even more arguable. If we do not know

the total population we can hardly expect to have such detail as this. The only parallels to apply are those of pre-industrial societies in Europe, where there is ample information. Detailed examination reveals continual fluctuation in the crude death rate, calculated in numbers per thousand, with occasional peaks caused by epidemics, chiefly plague. Also, even discounting the major outbreaks of plague, the death rates in towns seem to have been higher than in the country. In general, however, the death rate seems to have varied between 20 and 30 per thousand per year, but sometimes to have gone as high as 50 per thousand. Certainly anything less than 20 per thousand was very rare until the coming of industrialization (Wrigley 1969, 162-3, fig. 5.2). Thus to take a level of 25 per thousand seems if anything to be erring on the side of caution. It thus appears that the estimates of cemetery populations given above are by no means low.

Cemeteries of Roman Gaul

It must be considered how these millions of graves are represented in the archaeological record. The most difficult area of the western Empire is that contained now in modern France. The provinces of Gaul are central to any arguments about what was happening in the civil zones of the west. In Gallia Belgica we are exceptionally well provided with burial evidence, especially through the work of van Doorselaer (1964, 1967), and the reports on the cemeteries at Blicquy and Wederath (de Laet et al. 1972; Haffner 1971 and 1974). Here we have a full gazetteer of burial sites and extensive analysis and excavation reports of cemeteries. Elsewhere the position is not so happy. The last few years have seen several sites excavated on quite substantial scales, but without much systematic publication as yet. In Gallia Lugdunensis at Jublains (Mayenne) in north-west France, 124 cremation graves have been uncovered dating from the 1st and 2nd centuries (Gallia 1971, 249). Continuing work at Lezoux (Puy-de-Dôme) in central France is producing a large amount of material with great significance for the study of pottery as well as burial (Gallia 1973, 445-7; Partridge 1973). There is also still activity at Briord (Ain), north-east of Lyon, where excavations were conducted throughout the 1960s (Grange, Parriat, Perraud 1965; Gallia 1966, 485; 1968, 559; 1971, 407; 1973, 515). Now more than 370 graves have been found, spanning a long period from the 1st century through to the 7th; yet even in the 1st and 2nd centuries inhumation was significantly more popular than cremation. It will be very interesting to examine this site in detail when full information is available, as it provides an excellent example of a local centre with its own continuing practices. At Lyon we find an impressive total of more than 500 epitaphs (Audin and Burnand 1959), but this must seem slight in comparison with the estimate of graves given above. Many of the stones came from the cemetery of Trion. Dug in the last century, a substantial part of the cemetery had been buried in the 1st century AD, and so was remarkably well preserved. However, little is recorded in detail and we can only imagine what might have been revealed had the excavation been carried out and published under modern conditions, with improved standards and techniques (Audin 1965, 133-4). At Lyon cremation seems to have been dominant in the 1st century, with inhumation only appearing in the 2nd.

At Vienne (Isère), not far from Lyon, but in Gallia Narbonensis, a part of the town's main cemetery at Charavel has recently been dug. Only about 40 graves were in fact excavated, with none dating earlier than the 2nd century (*Gallia* 1971, 426). Although thoroughly excavated, such a small sample allows very little consideration of the cemetery as a whole. Unfortunately this is common throughout the province. Parts of cemeteries at Apt (Vaucluse), *Colonia Apta Julia*, and at La Calade, Cabasse (Var) have been dug and fully published, but they were limited to only 33 and 40 graves respectively (Apt: Dumoulin 1964, Barruol 1968; La Calade: Bérard 1961 and 1963), although a further 33 graves have now been excavated at Cabasse (*Gallia* 1973, 551-3). Such work is satisfactory only within very restricted limits. Only at Lattes (Hérault), near Montpellier, is there a site where enough graves have been excavated for there to be a chance of some substantial conclusions. Not only have more than 150 graves been found, but, giving almost an embarrassment of riches, there were also 34 gravestones, mostly still *in situ*. Some of these have already been discussed for their epigraphic interest (Demougeot 1972), but their full significance can only be seen when they are compared with the graves themselves and any patterns in the style of deposit can be discerned. It is already clear that the graves were generally elaborately furnished (*Gallia* 1966, 467-8; 1969, 394i; 1971, 381). Moreover there is perhaps some indication of the status of the people using this part of the cemetery in that the stones give no mention of any magistrates of the town. Of the 41 individuals mentioned by name on the stones, two were freedwomen and one a freedman, fifteen people had peregrine status (of whom at least twelve were of Gallic origin) and at least nineteen were citizens. This epigraphic evidence excludes two main sections of what we would expect to be the social structure of the town, the magistrates and the poor. There are enough graves apparently without stone grave markers to accommodate the poor, but we may be forced to conclude that the wealthiest groups of society used a special part of this cemetery as yet unsampled, or did not leave behind any gravestones, which seems unlikely, or were buried outside the main cemetery, possibly elsewhere round the town or else on their country estates. The proportion of expensively marked graves in this sample, about 1 in 5, may have been distorted but does seem to be in the sort of range that might be expected. The material already available from Lattes begins to show the kind of evidence that can be hoped for from substantial excavation of cemeteries, and whets the appetite not only for the final report on this site itself, but also for more extensive work on others in the area. Several lines of enquiry can be discerned for further study in Gallia Narbonensis, such as the frequency of the occurrence of cists, sometimes of tile, sometimes of stone. Cylindrical stone cists, with the cavity cut out from a solid drum, seem to have been popular on several sites, notably at Apt, at Tavel (Gard) (Gagnière et al. 1961), and even as far away as in Haut-Vienne (Perrier 1964, pl. VI). Such distinctive practices, or fashions, deserve full consideration, examining their distribution both generally in the province and in particular cemeteries. Similarly the excavators of the cremation cemetery at Saze (Gard) noticed a gap in use in the 3rd century, following a decline in numbers in the 2nd before a resumption of burial in the 4th, now by inhumation (Gagnière and Granier 1972). They claim that

such a break is common elsewhere in the lower Rhône valley. This clearly needs more study, if only to ensure that the dating evidence for these gaps is generally convincing. What the implications for the 3rd century might be, if it is, is another matter. It may be related to changes in burial practice with the adoption of inhumation. Only by thorough work will it emerge how many centres with a continuing local tradition like Briord there may be.

The classification of graves

The picture in France is thus very sketchy. Several large graveyards have been dug in recent years, but none have yet been fully reported; final accounts have only appeared for very small samples. Some classifications have been attempted already, but they usually fail to account satisfactorily for all the variation immediately observable even within that one cemetery.

One recent attempt at typology in the report on the cemetery at Blicquy in Belgium distinguished first the type of grave (simple, in a wooden box, in a stone cist, or in a tile cist); second, whether there was an urn present or not; and third, whether the ashes were all concentrated together or were dispersed (de Laet et al. 1972, A, 21-3). While covering the actual grave quite satisfactorily, this system does not take into account the composition of the grave goods. Another method appeared in a preliminary report on the excavation of the cemetery at Jublains (*Gallia* 1971, 249). Four types were noted here: cremations with no associations (10 graves); cremations in wooden boxes (5 graves); cremations without an actual container, but with a pot covering the ashes on the ground (2 graves); cremations in a pottery urn (102 graves) or in a glass urn (5 graves), with or without food vessels, either beakers or flagons. This last type again pays little attention to the grave goods and is hardly a cohesive unit.

A comprehensive classification of the burial practices distinguished in ethnographic studies can only be of general interest here, as it would tend to group all Roman burials together, being similar in fundamentals, and so ignore the variation of detail that is our main concern (Sprague 1968). Yet there is room for much variation in the several aspects by which any grave can be described: the nature and treatment of the corpse itself, the type of grave given it, and the composition of any grave goods. To make any sort of sense of this it is essential to consider the evidence over a very wide span of examples, in order to find out what has any meaning for significant numbers of graves. France provides very marked support for this, since vast numbers of isolated graves have been found over the years and summarily recorded, but they are of very little use in any serious attempt to discover patterns in the funerary evidence. There is almost bound to be a distortion in recovery favouring richer graves. Without a broad field of study, ideally of complete cemeteries, it is impossible to see such stray finds in their true context.

Quantitative studies

If these arguments for a comprehensive study of cemeteries, as opposed to individual graves, are accepted, we are confronted with an immediate, purely practical problem of dealing with all the material required. It is the present writer's opinion that a computer provides the simplest and most convenient means of doing this.

In some disciplines this might need no defence, but some doubt has been expressed by archaeologists that it is often more of a gimmick than a necessary tool. Some people may well have been frightened away by mathematics and statistics, and, perhaps with more justification, have felt a resistance to the specialized jargon of some computer scientists. Nevertheless, the capacity of the computer to sort and analyse a large quantity of information must force us to overcome such distastes and make determined attempts to understand what computers can do for us and equally what they cannot. No alternative method of dealing with such quantities of data can rival the computer's speed, simplicity and flexibility. The traditional approach to research of assembling evidence and recording it on a card index system and then depending on memory or intuition to find significant patterns has very obvious and often noted shortcomings. Even if all the steps in the process operate with the greatest efficiency and the researcher has a magnificent memory, there is still a strong likelihood that elements will be overlooked and that the final result will too strongly reflect his personal preconceptions. This is particularly a danger when the evidence consists of a mass of small details or occurrences. The present writer certainly does not feel equipped to depend on his own memory when considering more than 5000 graves.

There have been other ways tried of achieving a more thorough system without going as far as the computer. A recent study of Gallo-Roman graves in Limousin adopted a simple graphic approach, which has the estimable asset of presenting the information in a form which is immediately accessible to the eye (Mennessier 1973). As at present published, this considers 62 attributes of each grave and is applied to a total of only 103 graves. The approach can undoubtedly be welcomed, but there are important limitations to this method. Firstly it is rather inflexible in assessing the possible correlations even on this sample. The method consists of constructing a table with the individual graves on one axis and the 62 attributes on the other. The presence of each attribute is plotted in each grave using small counters shaded to show different intensities of occurrence. Correlations are achieved by physically manipulating these graphs, set up on a sort of board. For publication the arrangements considered significant can be photographed. On relatively simple material this system can prove effective, since the basic sorting can be done by eye very quickly and the results are apparent at once. Essentially the manipulator is doing the same job as the computer would, using much more complex mathematical measures of similarity. Yet it remains strongly subjective and the problems created by trying to achieve a really detailed analysis by this means with many more examples are quickly evident.

The kind of difficulty is well illustrated in the 'Analysis of Graves' presented as a table in the report on the Romano-British cemetery at St Pancras, Chichester (Down and Rule 1971, 71). It tells how often various characteristics of the graves, such as Samian pottery or mirrors occurred, but gives no indication of how often they appeared together in the same graves. The degree of subtlety required in such a consideration of the grave goods makes thoroughly unwieldy at the very best any attempt to draw up on paper a table that can take account of all the variations possible. One example of the problems met in this method is that it is difficult to relate the descriptions of grave goods in terms of function and of material: it is bound to be cumbersome to compare the presence of objects made of bronze and those of fine pottery, at the same time as any correlations between flagons and brooches. It is so much easier to make the computer perform that kind of task, which is what it was designed to do.

At least these methods and any computer-based system demand a more rigorous attitude to the evidence. One must be aware at all times of exactly what are the attributes that are being compared. Only if the material being used has the potential of providing some sound conclusion is the enterprise worthwhile. To describe an artifact, whether it be a brooch or a stone axe, only in terms of simple measurements and ratios, however carefully or objectively chosen, can only produce a typology based on morphology. It is probably some advance on a traditional intuitive classification, in that it does make plain what the criteria are, but it is a limited one, for it still excludes many other factors, such as context or usage, which are perhaps more likely to be meaningful than just shape. To take such morphological data and put them in a computer in no way improves them; computer analysis can never change the nature of the evidence. On this point graves have some advantage over simple artefacts, since it is possible to distinguish definite presences of objects placed in the grave and fairly clear types of grave, relieving the worried researcher of having to decide what basic dimensions are likely to be significant, and allowing him simply to record all he can about the graves. This makes the raw material compatible to computer analysis, as it can be done mainly on the basis of presences. Much of the success of the operation will depend on the system of coding used, for the machine can only work with what it is told through this medium.

A coding system for Roman graves

As the quality of evidence recorded from different excavations varies considerably, the system of coding devised for this research is confined to the evidence which is virtually always noted: the nature and treatment of the corpse itself, the type of grave, and the composition of any grave goods. This undoubtedly excludes a great deal of evidence that might be available from the best excavations, such as orientation, groupings of graves, depths, and careful analyses of the soils and the cremated bones. Yet to restrict this study to those few excavated cemeteries that can offer even some of these tempting items would mean to abandon it. Valuable results can come from looking at the material now available which may stimulate further work in the field, perhaps of a higher standard. Moreover, where some of this additional information is available, such as the spatial groupings shown on the plan of a cemetery, it must later be compared with the groupings found in the main computer analysis, even though this extra information was not originally involved in those analyses.

The first category of the main evidence is the nature of the corpse. This mostly concerns its age and sex; in practice it is largely limited to inhumation graves, because so few cremations have been fully examined. Although too often even the inhumations have not received adequate anatomical study, it is usually recorded whether the skeleton is that of a child or an adult. It is possible that the body was buried wearing clothes or shoes, or was wrapped in a shroud, or had been given some other preparation for the grave. After this, the principal question is whether or not the corpse was cremated. Inhumation is general, even for cremations, since most were indeed buried in the ground. The only exceptions that we can normally recognize are those where the body is placed in some sort of monument above the ground. The remains were often placed in a vessel, but here a distinction must be made between the container itself, holding only the human remains, and the coffin holding the whole deposit, including any grave goods. This distinction is sometimes rather difficult, especially when the grave is a simple inhumation in a wooden box without **grave goods, yet it is at its clearest with cremations**. In practice containers can rarely be identified in simple inhumations.

The body, however prepared, must then be disposed of, usually in the ground if the grave has been found by archaeology. The grave may be no more than a plain trench, but it may be elaborated by having a cist of tile or stone to enclose the interment. We must then consider whether the grave was marked on the surface in any special way beyond the small mound of disturbed earth.

As for the grave goods, it may have been observed that they have been treated in some peculiar way, for example arranged in neat groups or turned upside down. It is clearly hard to decide whether such visible patterns are more than just accident, yet it is quite conceivable that they were regarded as the most important part of the ritual, and they must therefore be recorded. Finally, the items that make up any grave furniture should be noted as to their functions, materials, and number. Most of these points are fairly self-evident, but some problem does appear over the functional description of pottery, which is the most common grave-find, since its classification has not been altogether standardized. As far as possible the distinctions given by Webster (1969, 8-11) are followed here, but inevitably this is sometimes subjective. The individual classes of vessel have been grouped further by general function; for example, flagons, jugs, and bottles are all linked as vessels for the storage of liquid. For present purposes this arrangement seemed more likely to produce meaningful comparisons, at the admitted cost of some loss of precision.

These are the elements of the evidence that must be examined to find any significant correlations. The coding system was designed to deal with a specific research problem and it is hoped that it copes with the mass of data neatly and conveniently. The most straighforward method would have been to make a comprehensive check-list of all the possible attributes of a grave and to have ticked off each one as it occurred. This has the major advantage of providing an elementary visual representation of the patterns, showing those attributes which are often found together. Its overwhelming drawbacks, however, are the large number of possible attributes needing space for entries, most of which would be used only occasionally, if at all, and the general lack of flexibility in manipulating the information. For the present work it was decided that it was much better to let the computer do the work of compiling and manipulating the equivalent of such a chart, and to this end a system was devised which only allowed for data entries where a particular attribute was present in a grave. Geoff Wright of the Computer Centre at University College, London, wrote a programme to convert the data as written down into a form acceptable to the CLUSTAN programmes that were to be used. This programme freed the coding system from restraints other than those of clarity, convenience and accuracy.

For the purposes of coding the observed attributes were separated into two groups, functional and descriptive. The full list of attributes is given in the Appendix (p. 25). There are certainly some inconsistencies in the functional attributes in that two of them, the date (02) and the type of grave (15), are, without the qualification of a descriptive attribute, little more than labels. The evidence for the date of an individual grave is, however, often so unreliable that it is not intended here to be included in the main computer analyses. Similarly, the question of whether or not the grave has been disturbed is not intended for

inclusion (01); its purpose is to permit the exclusion of contaminated evidence. The type of grave is certainly of greater significance and could lead to distortion if used without the descriptive attributes attached to it. The other attributes from 03 to 16 can, if necessary, be used to effect without extra description. The remaining functional attributes all refer to grave-goods and may be of some significance on their own, on a simple presence or absence basis.

The descriptive attributes cover a variety of evidence and mostly amplify the information recorded. The first group concerns the date brackets, which can practically be no more accurate than at intervals of 50 years. Next are the various possible ways in which the body has been prepared, the type of grave, and the condition and arrangement of the grave-goods. Finally comes the list of materials, which can apply to the container, the coffin, or the grave goods. The material recorded for a composite object is the one predominant in its construction. Here the only distinction noted in the pottery is between coarse and fine wares. This undoubtedly ignores much detailed information, but unfortunately most of this information is not comparable from province to province in any more significant way, whereas the distinction made does attempt **to show whether the vessel was expensive or cheap. In** some provinces it is a problem where to draw the line between coarse and fine wares, but generally the criterion adopted is that fine wares include imported or widely traded wares and any others which can be seen as the best table wares. In both the functional and the descriptive attributes some coding provision has been made in the form of 'other' categories for items that are not included in the main lists, so that any unusual occurrences are recorded in the coding, even if not in detail.

Some typical coded graves are given in the Appendix. They are usually recorded on computer data forms and then punched on to cards. The first part of the entry for each grave is its identification label, giving the cemetery in a three-letter code, followed by the grave number within the cemetery. The attributes are then noted, but not in any particular order, so that items can be added out of numerical sequence if first omitted. The entry for each separate attribute present takes six spaces. The first space gives the number of items conforming to the description which follows. In the rare cases where more than nine examples of an item are involved the count is left at nine and merely indicates that a large number of examples is present. This part of the entry is often not applicable, as for instance with the attributes cremation and inhumation (11, 12); in such cases the entry must be made as 0. This column is thus significant only when a number greater than 0 is registered. The second and third spaces are used for the functional attributes, which, for ease of reading, are separated by a stop from the descriptive attributes in the fifth and sixth spaces. Where no descriptive attribute is applicable, the entry must still be completed by the notation .00. Since the functional and descriptive attributes always occupy the same relative positions in each entry, it is simple to arrange runs which will consider either one separately or both together, with or without the number of items.

This coding system has been described in some detail, but with no intention of persuading other archaeologists studying burials to adopt it. On the contrary, this system is only designed to deal with the particular needs of one programme of research. As such it can be of no more than indirect interest to other workers. The aim of presenting it here is to outline the nature of the evidence in Roman burials and to show the beginnings of a classification of at least the categories of material. By stressing the coding it is hoped to emphasize the importance, when trying to use statistical techniques and computers, of being aware of exactly what information is being compared and investigated for significant correlations. Only if the coding is as sound and comprehensive as possible can the results obtained from the analysis be worthwhile.

Conclusions

The choice of actual programmes to use on these data is another crucial decision. Many different techniques are available and it is important to find the most suitable. So far on this project the primary technique has been cluster analysis, which sorts the units of data into groups of the most similar on the basis of a number of varying attributes; here the units are graves and the attributes are grave goods and descriptions of the grave and corpse. The process is carried on at various levels of similarity (for discussion of cluster analysis on archaeological material see Doran & Hodson 1975; Hodson 1970 and 1971; Rowlett and Pollnac 1971). This does not necessarily tell which attributes occur so frequently together that they can be distinguished as a 'type' and a separate analysis of the attributes themselves is required for this. It is important for the archaeologist using these techniques to understand their basic principles, if he is to avoid making a fool of himself by giving quite the wrong interpretations to his computed results, merely through ignorance. Many archaeologists working with computers have had their own special programmes written. Whilst this is extremely useful in developing the techniques available, it seemed to me that the archaeologist with all his other distractions can rarely hope to become a proficient computer scientist as well, and that, if computers are to be used as widely and successfully as I hope they will, we must try to make use of the various library programmes and packages of programmes which have been developed and do seem to satisfy many other disciplines and even industry beyond the academic world. It certainly seemed worth trying what could be used at once without having to start from scratch. If we are to realize the full potential of computers in archaeology they must be available to those who seek specifically archaeological conclusions. Here concern with the techniques involved is limited to their direct relation to the results produced, rather than the intricacies of detail in the programmes. Although there are obvious dangers in this, it seems to me that we must ultimately put our trust in the computer scientists and lean heavily on their advice, as archaeologists freely do with specialists in other related disciplines. The only part of the programmes specially written for this work is that by Geoff Wright to convert the coded data into a form acceptable to the CLUSTAN package used for the main analysis.

It should not be thought that computing is an easy option, allowing the archaeologist to sit back and let the machine do all the work. In many ways it is more demanding than traditional methods. It frees us from a deal of tedious calculation, but enables us to turn our minds to more rewarding stuff. One process that cannot be avoided is the systematic examination of all the evidence for coding. This is perhaps likely to be even more thorough than in conventional research. Indeed, doing it all oneself may well suggest patterns that will bear further examination later. Yet the main work is going through the results of the programmes as printed out. In a cluster analysis this will involve the tracing back of how the clusters have developed at different levels of similarity and

finding out which levels may correlate with such factors as chronology or place of origin. Also the attributes which are the characteristics of each cluster must be looked at. There are also various ways of presenting the results, in tables, dendrograms, graphs, or scatter diagrams, which must all be explored to see if they reveal something concealed before. It can be seen that to some extent this allows the evidence to follow its own logic and the computer to decide which questions to ask of it. If the programme is working satisfactorily it should in fact select which are the best groupings to choose and the best attributes to split existing clusters. If the behaviour of some particular set of attributes or examples is thought to be of special interest it can be followed through the results printed out, or even special runs can be arranged to investigate it. It may also be that the computer is not big enough to take all the examples at once. If so sets of evidence must be selected to show the whole from all sorts of different angles. It may be rewarding to compare the groupings found within a single cemetery with those in a sample randomly chosen from several. At least all the effort put in on the results is involving dynamic evidence; it is a question of considering many possible interpretations of the evidence. Many of these will have to be discarded, but they are still important as stimuli to thought.

Throughout the emphasis should be on the opportunities that the computer can provide. It can free us of a mass of calculations and analytical drudgery. Certainly little is lost by its use, since there is nothing from traditional methods that is prevented by it. It allows us to widen the scope of our researches enormously. Yet convincing proof of the techniques can only come from sound results. At the time of writing those from this study are tentative but there is more than enough promise in them to be hopeful.

References

Audin, A (1965) *Lyon, miroir de Rome dans les Gaules* (Paris)
Audin, A, and Burnand, Y (1959) 'Chronologie des épitaphes romaines de Lyon' *Rev. Etudes Anc.* **61,** 320-52
Barruol, G (1968) 'Essai sur la topographie d'Apta Julia' *Rev. Archéol Narbonnaise* **1,** 101-58
Bérard, G (1961) 'La nécropole gallo-romaine de La Calade à Cabasse (Var)' *Gallia* **19,** 105-58
Bérard, G (1963) 'La nécropole gallo-romaine de La Calade à Cabasse (Var). Deuxième campagne de fouilles (1962)' *ibid* **21,** 295-306
de Laet, S J, van Doorselaer, A, Spitaels, P, and Thoen, H (1972) *La Nécropole Gallo-Romaine de Blicquy* (Dissertationes Archaeologicae Gandenses **14**)
Demougeot, E (1972) 'Stèles funéraires d'une nécropole de Lattes' *Rev. Archéol. Narbonnaise* **5,** 49-116
Doran, J E, and Hodson, F R (1975) *Mathematics and Computers in Archaeology* (Edinburgh University Press)
Down, A, and Rule, M (1971) *Chichester Excavations* **1** (Chichester)
Dumoulin, A (1964) 'Découverte d'une nécropole gallo-romaine à Apt' *Gallia* **22,** 87ff
Duncan-Jones, R P (1974) *The Economy of the Roman Empire*
Gagnière, S, Granier, J, and Perrot, R (1961) 'Sépultures à incinération de la première siècle à Tavel (Gard)' *Gallia* **19,** 232-43
Gagnière, S, and Granier, J (1972) 'La nécropole gallo-romaine et barbare de la Font-du-Buis à Saze (Gard)' *Rev. Archéol. Narbonnaise* **5,** 117-44
Gallia (1966) 'Informations archéologiques', **24,** 239ff
Gallia (1968) 'Informations archéologiques', **26,** 321ff
Gallia (1971) 'Informations archéologiques', **29,** 219ff
Gallia (1973) 'Informations archéologiques', **31,** 313ff
Grange, A, Parriat, H, and Perraud, R (1965) *La Nécropole Gallo-Romaine de Briord (Ain)* Société d'Archéologie de Briord et ses environs: edition de La Physiophile. Société des Sciences Naturelles et Historiques, Monceau-Les-Mines (Saône-et-Loire), 62
Haffner, A (1971/1974) *Das Keltisch-Römische Graberfeld von Wederath-Belginum* **1** (1971), **2** (1974)
Hodson, F R (1970) 'Cluster analysis and archaeology: some developments and applications' *World Archaeol.* **1,** 299-320
Hodson, F R (1971) 'Numerical typology and prehistoric archaeology' in Hodson, F R, Kendall, D G, and Tautu, P (eds) *Mathematics in the Archaeological and Historical Sciences,* 30-45 (Edinburgh University Press)

Mennessier, C (1973) 'Tombes gallo-romaines du Limousin: traitement graphiques de l'information' in Duval, P-M, et al *Recherches d'archéologie celtique et gallo-romaine* (Publications du Centre de Recherches d'Histoire et du Philologie, **3**—Hautes études du monde gréco-romain **5**: Geneva), 83-95

Partridge, C (1973) 'Lezoux 1973' *Hertfordshire Archaeol.* **8**, 143-4

Perrier, J (1964) *Carte Archéologique de la Gaule Romaine*, **14**, *Haute-Vienne* (Paris)

Rowlett, R, and Pollnac, R B (1971) 'Multivariate analysis of Marnian La Tène cultural groups' in Hodson, F R, Kendall, D G, and Tautu, P (eds) *Mathematics in the Archaeological and Historical Sciences*, 46-58 (Edinburgh: University Press)

Sprague, R (1968) 'A suggested terminology and classification for burial description' *American Antiquity* **33** (4), 479-85

Ucko, P J (1969) 'Ethnography and the archaeological interpretation of funerary remains' *World Archaeol.* **1**, 262-80

van Doorselaer, A (1964) *Répertoire des Nécropoles d'Epoque Romaine en Gaule Septentrionale* (Brussels)

van Doorselaer, A (1967) *Les Nécropoles d'Epoque Romaine en Gaule Septentrionale* (Dissertationes Archaeologicae Gandenses **10**)

Webster, G (1969) *Romano-British Coarse Pottery: A Student's Guide* 2nd ed (London: Council for British Archaeology, Res. Rep. **6**)

Wheeler, Sir Mortimer (1956) *Still Digging* (London: Joseph)

Wrigley, E A (1969) *Population and History* (London)

Appendix

The coding system

A *Functional attributes*
01 Grave disturbed (either in ancient or modern times)
02 Date of grave
03 Single burial
04 Part of multiple burial
05 Child
06 Mature adult
07 Old adult (*c.* 45-50+)
08 Male
09 Female
10 Body preparations
11 Cremated
12 Inhumed
13 Container for corpse
14 Coffin
15 Grave type
16 State of grave-goods

Grave-goods present:
17 Brooches
18 Buckles
19 Bracelets
20 Beads
21 Needles/Pins
22 Rings
23 Lamps or lampstands
24 Mirrors
25 Toilet items
26 Boots or shoes
27 Belts
28 Weapons or tools
29 Meals or food remains
30 Eating utensils
31 Liquid storage vessels (flagons, flasks, bottles, etc.)
32 Drinking vessels (beakers, cups, etc.)
33 Eating vessels (dishes, bowls, plates, etc.)
34 Coins
35 Discs
36 Phials or unguent jars
37 Human figures or statuettes
38 Games or dice
39 Boxes
40 Fragments
41 Cooking or storage jars
42 Mortaria or food preparation vessels
43 Other vessels
44 Nails

45 Lids
46 Miniatures
47 Medical instruments
48 Inscriptions
49 Other personal ornaments
50 Other objects

B *Descriptive attributes*

Referring to	Number and description	
02	.01 before AD 1	.02 not before AD 1
	.03 not before AD 50	.04 not before AD 100
	.05 not before AD 150	.06 not before AD 200
	.07 not before AD 250	.08 not before AD 300
	.09 not before AD 350	.10 not before AD 400
	.11 not before AD 450	
10	.12 clothes on body	
	.13 coin with body itself (e.g. in mouth)	
	.14 gypsum or other coating on body	
	.15 shroud	
15	.16 plain trench	
	.17 cist of tile	
	.18 cist of stone	
	.19 marker visible above ground (stele, monument, etc.)	
	.20 pipe to surface for libations	
16	.21 grave-goods grouped at head of skeleton	
	.22 grave-goods grouped at middle of skeleton	
	.23 grave-goods grouped at feet of skeleton	
	.24 part or all of grave-goods inverted	
	.25 part or all of grave-goods wasters or seconds	
	.26 part or all of grave-goods broken deliberately	
13, 14, 17 to 50	.27 wood	.36 gold
	.28 glass	.37 iron
	.29 coarse pottery	.38 bone
	.30 fine pottery	.39 jet
	.31 amphora	.40 pewter
	.32 stone	.41 tin
	.33 lead	.42 leather
	.34 bronze	.43 terracotta
	.35 silver	.44 other material, or unknown

A typical grave recorded by this system would read as follows:
BLQ 176 001.00 002.03 003.00 011.00 012.00 113.30 015.16 217.34 133.29
STF 013 003.00 006.00 012.00 015.17
WED 430 003.00 011.00 012.00 015.16 141.29

Owslebury (Hants) and the problem of burials on rural settlements John Collis

An adequate knowledge of the development of burial customs during the Roman period can only be based on a large body of data, involving the extensive excavation of cemeteries as described elsewhere in this volume. There is inevitably a bias in this evidence, as large-scale cemetery excavation can only take place where there are concentrations of population as in the towns, and where there may be administrative, physical, or cultural pressures for the concentration of burials on specific plots of land assigned for that purpose. However, as I hope this paper will demonstrate, the situation is very different on the rural settlements, and the normal pattern is for burials to be scattered throughout the settlement area, sometimes almost at random. A large sample of burials is difficult to obtain, both for this reason, and because of the small size of the population. Owslebury still represents one of the most extensively excavated settlements, and I wish here to present a preliminary analysis prior to the final report which, owing to the large number of finds to be processed, will be some time in appearing. I hope also this paper will help redress the balance of this present volume.

The site

Owslebury lies some 5 miles (8 km) south-east of Winchester, near the southern edge of the chalk downs. It was under excavation for some twelve years between 1961 and 1972 through the generosity of the tenant farmer, Mr P J Hellard, and during this time about half of the main settlement area was excavated (Collis 1968, 1970, *Current Archaeology* **25,** 32-7). From the air it appears as a complex of ditches covering some 4-5 ha, a very common type of site in central Hampshire. Despite the size of the area, the settlement seems merely to have been a single farm, contrasting with village sites, which may cover 10-15 ha. The complexity is due in part to the longevity of the occupation, for it starts probably in the 3rd century BC and continues unbroken until the end of the 4th century AD.

The burials

In all 70 burials have been excavated, including two double burials, nos. 1 and 35. In addition there are a number of isolated human bones which have turned up with domestic rubbish, but these are not considered here. A preliminary list is given on Table I, incorporating information from Calvin Wells's study of the bones. The dates assigned are not yet definitive, nor the list of grave goods, which in some cases is based only on the original field notes.

There are three concentrations of burials which might be termed cemeteries (Figs. 1-4), though in only one case was there any formal layout:

Cemetery 1 (Fig. 5): Burials 7-13, 16-20, 35-39, 41, 44, 45. The cemetery is enclosed within two rectangular enclosures, themselves incorporated into a linear earthwork. The inhumation, burial 39, is likely to be the first burial,

lying near the centre of the earlier enclosure. Its grave-goods (Collis 1973), especially the shield-boss and the belt hook, can be closely paralleled among the finds supposedly found on the battlefield at Alesia, dating to 52 BC. All the remaining burials are cremations, the latest containing a samian vessel of Hadrianic date. Three inhumations which slight the enclosure ditch are presumably somewhat later and not connected.

Cemetery 2: Burials 28, 31, 65-68, probably 40, 51, 63, and possibly 27. These are all inhumations, only one in a coffin, cut into the fill of earlier ditches, which accounts for the linear layout. They are stratigraphically later than the 1st century BC; one is cut by a 3rd century ditch, and another by one of 4th century date. A 2nd century date is likely for the main cluster of burials.

Cemetery 3: Burials 29, 30, 32, 33, 42, 43, 46-49. This is a cemetery of infant burials cut into a ditch containing 1st century BC finds, but cut by one of 1st century AD date.

Of the other burials there are some obvious pairs: 5 and 6, 22 and 23, and 56 and 58, but the rest are generally scattered throughout the settlement area. One further burial should be mentioned, that of a young sheep which had broken a leg but had survived until the leg had healed. On its death it was provided with a 2nd century coin and a small pot, a quasi-human burial. Though a number of other complete animal skeletons were found, especially of dogs, none had been given such a careful burial.

Limitations of the data

One obvious limitation is the fact that only half of the settlement has been excavated. Though we have recently been exhorted to excavate these rural settlements completely, this is not easy with a complex site: 12 seasons of work try the patience of both farmer and director, and finances are not easy to obtain when sites fail to produce 'results' in the form of house structures. In any case burial often takes place on the fringe of the site, as is the case at Owslebury, though recent 'complete' excavations have often only concentrated on the main core of the settlement.

Secondly, the site has been heavily ploughed, and some burials may have completely disappeared. This is especially true of the Iron Age cemetery which was only discovered through the agency of the deep plough. Ploughing has also totally destroyed the bones of some burials in this cemetery, and often it can only be assumed that they were cremations. But in any case the amount of bone from some of the less disturbed cremations is so meagre that sex and age are impossible to establish. The majority of the excavated burials are on the north-facing slope where leaching and decomposition of the bones is at a maximum. Finally dating is very difficult for the later inhumation burials, none of which are given any grave-goods, and one usually has to rely on stratigraphical evidence, or horizontal relationships. The same problem is especially encountered with the infant burials.

TABLE I Burials from Owslebury.

No.	Date	Sex	Age	Burial rite	Grave goods
1	II AD	M+F	32± yrs	C in urn	36 + pots, bone inlays and pin (Figs. 9-11), animal and bird bones
3	I BC	—	0	I	none
4	?IV AD	—	foetus	I	none
5	III AD	—	35-45 yrs	I in coffin	none
6	III AD	M	15-16 yrs	I in coffin	none
7	I BC	—	—	C?	2-3 vessels and animal bone
8	I AD	—	—	C?	6-7 vessels and a brooch
9	I AD	—	? Young adult	C in pit	8 vessels (Fig. 7)
10	I BC	—	Young adult	C in urn	11 vessels (Fig. 6)
11	I BC	?F	Young adult	C in pit	11 vessels (Fig. 8)
12	I BC	—	Adult	C in box?	4-5 vessels
13§	I AD	—	—	C?	3-4 vessels
14*	I AD	—	—	I	none
15	?	—	0	I	none
16§	I AD	—	—	C?	2-3 vessels
17§	I BC	—	? Adult	I/C?	2-3 vessels
18§	II AD	—	—	C?	2-3 vessels, including a samian bowl
19	I AD	M	Adult	C in pit	2 pedestal jars, a platter, and an iron object
20§	I AD	—	—	C?	platter and samian cup
20a	?I AD	—	9-12 mths	I	none
21	?	—	12-18 mths	I	none
22	II AD	?M	30-50 yrs	I in coffin	none
23	II AD	—	17-18 yrs	I in coffin	none
24	?I AD	F	35-45 yrs	I crouched	none
25	?I BC	—	10-12 mths	I	none
26	III-IV AD	—	22-26 mths	I extended	none
27	?II-III AD	—	45-60 yrs	I flexed	none
28	?II-III AD	M	Adult	I in coffin	none
29	I BC	—	0	I	none
30	I BC	—	0	I	none
31	I-III AD	M	35-45 yrs	I extended	none
32	I BC	—	0	I	none
33	I BC	—	0	I	none
34	III AD	—	4-5 mths	I	none
35	IV AD	M+—	Adult + child	C in urn	urn + 3-4 vessels
36§	I BC	—	—	C?	1-2 vessels
37§	I BC	—	—	C?	1-2 vessels
38	I BC	—	? Adult	C	2 vessels
39	I BC	M	40-50 yrs	I extended	sword, spear, shield, belthook
40	II AD+	M	40-50 yrs	I flexed	none
41	I AD	M	Adult	C in pit	12 + vessels, razor, pig jaw
42	I BC	—	0	I	none
43	I BC	—	4-6 wks	I	none
44	I BC	—	—	C	1 vessel
45	I AD	M	Adult	C in pit	5 samian vessels, 2 flagons, 3 brooches
46	I BC	—	0	I	none
47	I BC	.	0	I	none
48	I BC	—	6 mths	I	none
49	I BC	—	0	I	none
50	?I BC	—	0	I	none
51	II AD+	M	35-50 yrs	I extended	none
52	?	—	0	I	none
53	?	—	?	I	none
54	?	—	0	I	none
55	IV AD	—	3-4 mths	I	none
56*	II-III BC	—	infant	I	none
57	IV AD	M	14-15 yrs	I extended	none
58*	II-III BC	—	infant	I	none
59	I AD	—	4-6 mths	I	none
60§	?	—	adult	I	none
61	?	—	0	I	none
62§	I BC	—	infant	I	none
63	?II AD	M	35-50 yrs	I flexed	none
64	I BC	—	0	I	none
65	II AD	M	35-45 yrs	I extended	none
66	II AD	—	20-22 mths	I flexed?	none
67	II AD	M	25-35 yrs	I flexed	brooch, fortuitous?
68	II AD	M	25-35 yrs	I flexed	none
69	I-II BC	—	1-2 yrs	C in pit	2 broken pots, burnt glass bead, and bangle
70*	?I BC	—	infant	I	none
—	II AD	—	sheep	I	1 vessel, coin

*   Full report on bones not yet received
§   Burial almost destroyed by ploughing
I   Inhumation
C   Cremation

Population size

The burial evidence falls fairly neatly into two: infants and children under 2, and adults of 15-16 plus. The age of about seventeen of the adults can be established approximately, and these suggest an average age at death of just over 34—near enough to 33.3 for my calculations! The most complete data on numbers of burials over a given period of time come from the Late La Tène/early Roman cemetery, with the addition of one possible 'poor' inhumation on the settlement. Over a period of just over 150 years there are twenty burials, one burial every 7½ years, and 13-14 a century. Assuming (perhaps rashly) that these were all burials of adults, this gives an adult population of about four or five at one time, two families.

On Fig. 12 I have taken the figure of fourteen adult burials per century and assumed that this remained static throughout the life of the settlement, though there are some grounds to argue for a smaller population in the 3rd and 2nd centuries BC, but as we have no burials for these periods anyway, the hypothesis cannot be tested. I have also assumed an infant mortality in the first two years of 30%, giving five infants per century, and a total of nineteen burials per century. The theoretical grand total of burials would be about 133, so in theory we have located over half of the expected bodies. It has not been possible to include a number of the burials as the dating evidence is too vague, and also unsexed adult burials have been divided evenly between male and female for each period. The expected bodies which have not been found are signified by a cross.

A glance at the chart shows that a large number of the missing bodies belong to the first two and a half centuries of occupation—the 'disappearing dead' of the Woodbury Culture. To judge by the one regular burial of this period, burial 69, which consisted of only a few scraps of burnt bone and crushed and scattered remains of two pots and a bangle, burials would be easy to miss. The other gap is

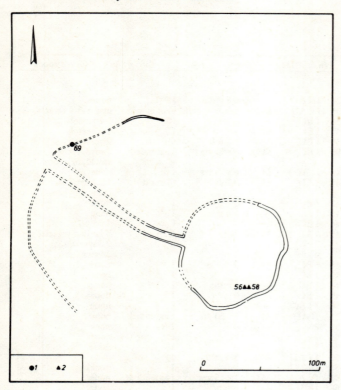

1   Plans and burials—2nd and 3rd centuries BC: 1. child burial;
    2. infant burials

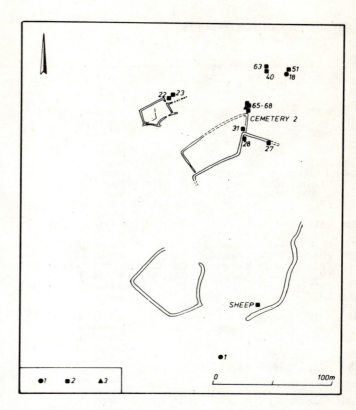

3   Plan and burials—2nd century AD: 1. cremations; 2. inhumations;
    3. infant burials

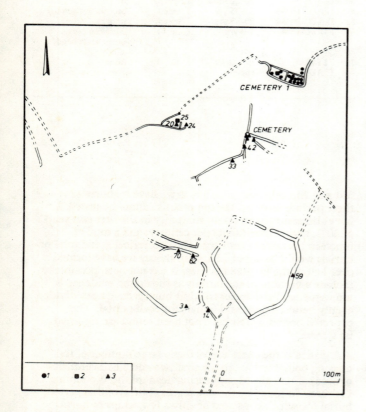

2   Plan and burials—1st century BC and 1st century AD: 1. adult
    burials; 2. infant burials; 3. age unknown

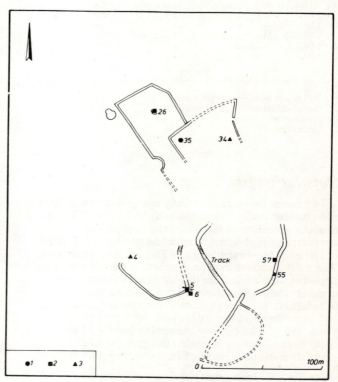

4   Plan and burials—3rd and 4th centuries AD: 1. cremations;
    2. inhumations; 3. infant burials

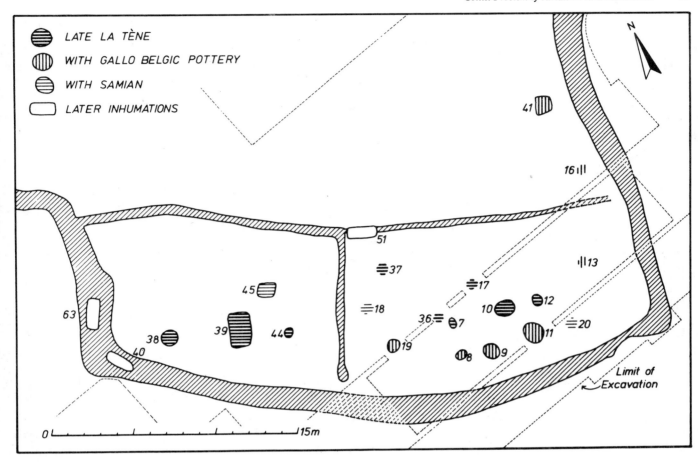

LATE LA TÈNE

WITH GALLO BELGIC POTTERY

WITH SAMIAN

LATER INHUMATIONS

5   *Late La Tène and early Roman cemetery*

for the latter part of the Roman period, especially female burials, and there may well be a cemetery somewhere awaiting excavation.

Two anomalies stand out. The first is the high incidence of infant burials in the 1st century BC, and they probably belong mainly to its second half, a mortality rate of about 60%. Of the fourteen for which an age has been established, all except three were newborn. In considering the total collection of infants from the site, Calvin Wells writes 'Infant deaths are commonly due to such infections as dysentery and enteritis, as a result of drinking contaminated cow's milk when maternal lactation fails. But deaths from these diseases occur very commonly, at least throughout the first five or six years of childhood, whereas the fact that of the 25 deaths under the age of 2 years, seventeen appeared to be newborn must make one wonder if the likeliest explanation is infanticide'.

The second anomaly is the large number of male burials and lack of females in the later Roman period (13 male, 2 female), and especially the overhigh number of males in the 2nd century. This could be in part due to the difficulty of dating, and some of the burials could well be 3rd century. However the lack of females is significant, as the burials occur in groups of two (twice), three, and five, and in the latter case at least the lack of a woman or two is surprising. There are two obvious hypotheses: either the

women were buried elsewhere, or there was a preponderance of men on the site.

The burial rite

There are five burials of children of one year or above. Of these two were cremated (35 and 69), one was an extended inhumation in an adult-sized grave (26), and a fourth (66) had been buried in an adult cemetery. Only one burial over 12 months (though less than 18 months) was apparently treated as an infant (21). It would seem that throughout the occupation of the site that children from at least 18 months were accorded adult status in burial, perhaps roughly corresponding with the age of walking and talking. These four burials will be included in the analysis that follows.

A summary of the burial rites is shown on Fig. 13. Each cross denotes an individual, so the two double burials 1 and 35 are represented by two crosses each. Cremation seems to have been practised at all periods, except perhaps the earliest, for which we have no evidence. In the earliest cremation (69) the bones were scattered in the fill of the grave, as also in the six diagnostic graves of 1st century AD date. Urn burial occurs in the 1st century BC and in the two later Roman burials.

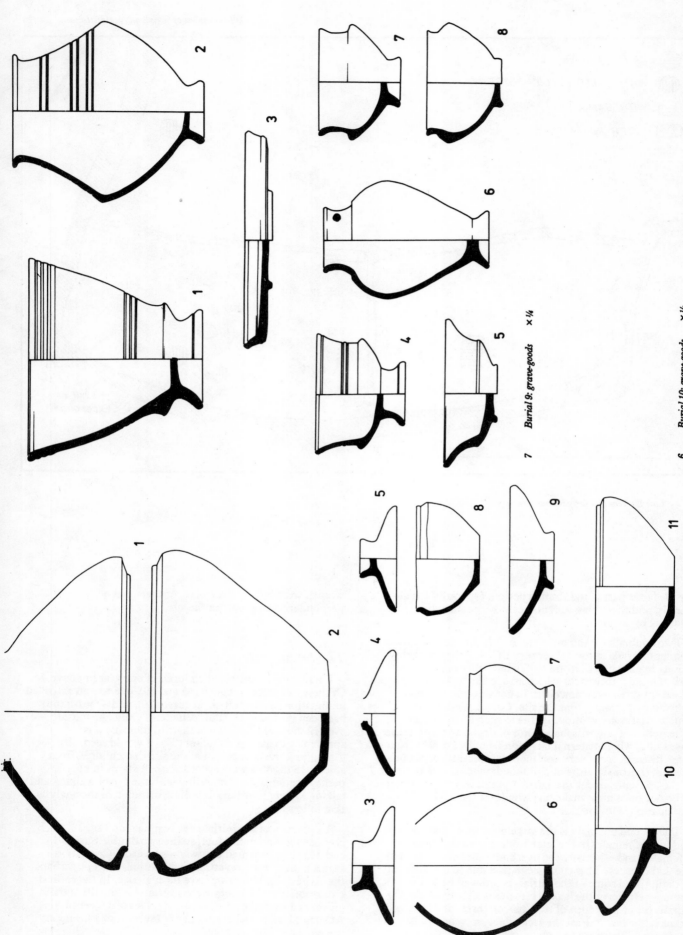

Burial 9: grave-goods   × ¼

Burial 10: grave-goods   × ¼

30

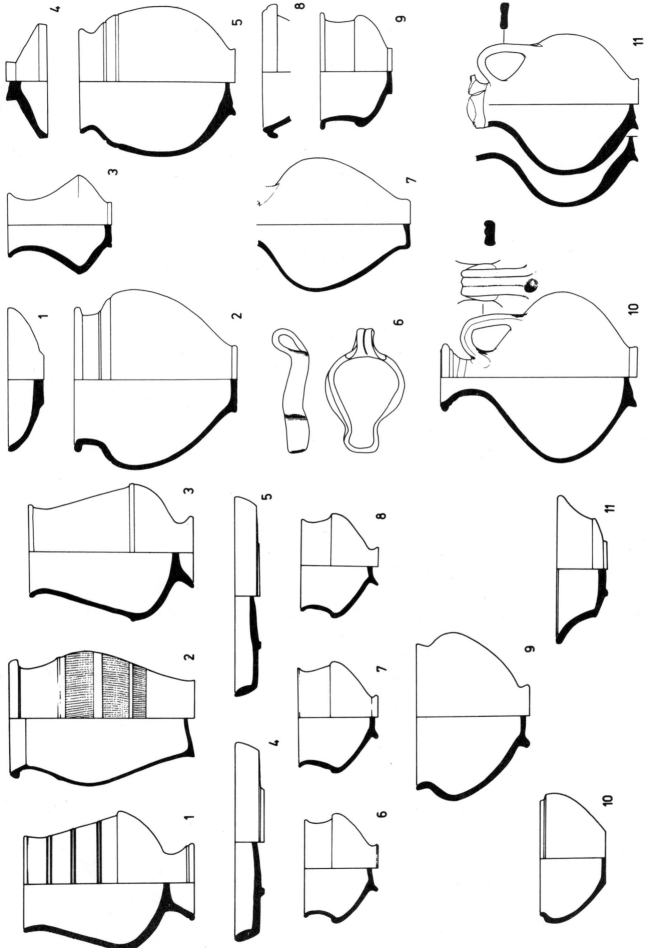

9   Burial 1: urn (no. 2) and accessory vessels   × ¼

8   Burial 11: grave-goods   × ¼

31

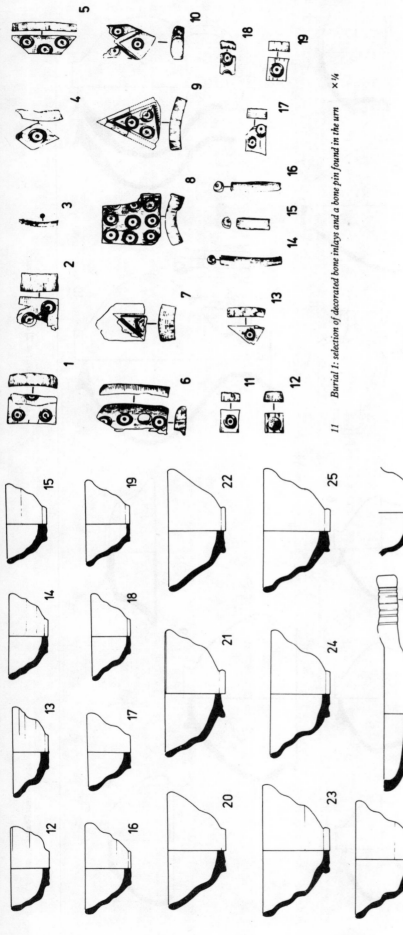

11 *Burial 1: selection of decorated bone inlays and a bone pin found in the urn* × ¼

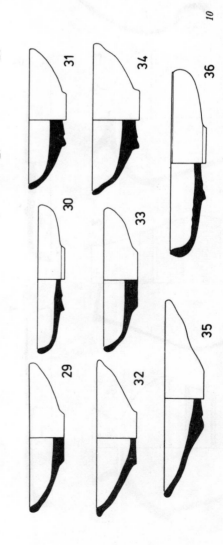

10 *Burial 1: accessory vessels deliberately made for burial* × ¼

32

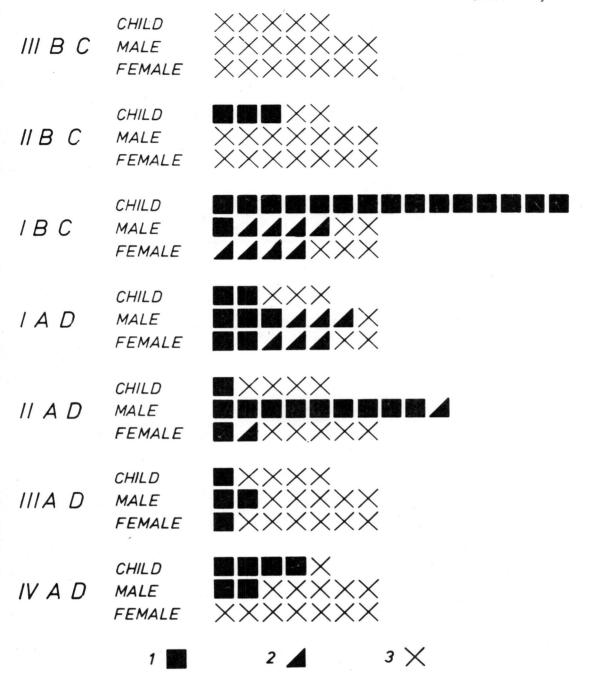

12   *Comparison of hypothetical number of burials per century with those actually found: 1. sexed burials and infant burials; 2. unsexed burials; 3. burials not discovered*

The inhumations I have divided into three groups. First, there are the coffin burials—in the heavily wormed chalk soil only detectable by the presence of nails. Secondly, there are flexed, crouched, or otherwise disarranged bodies, which could not have been enclosed in coffins. Often the layout of the body is careless: in one case the corpse lay on its face. Some could have been buried in shrouds, but most are too disarranged even for this. The third group are less diagnostic, being simple extended inhumations, and so could have had plain wooden coffins, but generally they are in close association with the irregular inhumations. Burial 39, both by its date and the presence of grave-goods, is entirely exceptional. None of the other inhumations had grave-goods, not even hob-nailed boots as is common at Winchester. This may however be due entirely to the lack of late Roman burials when this rite was most widespread.

Cremation, coffin, and irregular burials all occur alongside one another from the 2nd century AD.

	CREMATIONS	INHUMATION IN COFFIN	EXTENDED INHUMATION	IRREGULAR INHUMATION
II B.C.	X			
I B.C.	XXXXXXX		X	
I A.D.	XXXXXXXX			X
II A.D.	XXX	XXX	XXX	XXXXX
III A.D.		XX		X
IV A.D.	XX		XX	

13   *Occurrence of burial rites per century*

Interpretation

The evidence divides itself into three main phases.

1: The *earliest phase* runs from the foundation of the settlement in the 3rd or 4th century BC until the middle of the 1st century BC, corresponding with the 'banjo' enclosure, and the beginning of the multiple-ditched trackway phase. Other than two infant burials in the same storage pit, there is only one burial, the child cremation 69, which belongs somewhere towards the end of the phase. Little can be said about this period.

2: The *second period* runs from about 60-40 BC up to AD 120-130. It corresponds mainly with the multiple-ditched trackway phase, though the tracks were falling into disuse towards the end of the 1st century AD. This was a wealthy period, as shown both by the grave-goods, and by the number of gold and silver objects and coins which have been found on the settlement, the latest being a *denarius* of Trajan. However there may have been a recession in the second half of the 1st century BC with the collapse of the Hengistbury trade network, and before the appearance of the Colchester network, and it may be of significance that the majority of infant burials belong to this period. The majority of the population were cremated and buried in the enclosed cemetery, though there is one possible 'poor inhumation', hinting at the presence of a slave element. The adult population numbered at least four or five, presumably an extended family.

3: The *third phase* runs from the beginning of the 2nd century AD until the end of the Roman period, during which time two or three distinct social groups can perhaps be detected. First there are the rich cremations accompanied by many grave-goods (burials 1 and 35), secondly the coffin burials, and thirdly the irregular burials, the last two classes being predominated by males.

The implications seem to be a change in ownership with the abandonment of the cemetery, and a change in the social structure, with a single 'rich' family, and a lower class of labourers or slaves. That the inhumations were low-class burials is supported by Calvin Wells's study of the bones: 'The total impression is that these people led a very demanding life, under severe physical pressure from work and from their environment, which was further aggravated by personal aggression within the community'.

Conclusions

Despite the limitations of the material, one or two important hypotheses have emerged which it should be possible to test using chance finds and material from partial excavation of similar sites. But clearly more major excavations must take place before one can accept the Owslebury evidence as typical. One wonders for instance how comparable would be the burials for a site with a stone-built villa, and whether the changes we have noted at Owslebury and interpreted in social terms, may not merely reflect a universal trend in burial rites which one would find on town sites as well. But one lesson for those digging rural settlements is clear: the fringe areas of the settlement cannot be ignored, as that is where the majority of burials seem to be concentrated.

References

Collis, J R (1968) 'Excavations at Owslebury, Hants: an interim report' *Antiq. J.* **48**, 18-31
Collis, J R (1970) 'Excavations at Owslebury, Hants: a second interim report' *ibid* **50**, 246-61
Collis, J R (1973) 'Burials with weapons in Iron Age Britain' *Germania* **51**, 121-33

Pagan religions and burial practices in Roman Britain

Jock Macdonald

This essay tries to shed some light on the general beliefs and ideas about the afterlife which lay behind the material remains to be excavated in a Romano-British cemetery. It is the result of some of the questions that had to be posed during the excavation of a part of a 4th century cemetery at Lankhills School outside Winchester's North Gate. [1]

Three main traditions of religious experience were to be found in Britain during the Roman occupation: the Celtic, the Roman, and the Oriental. All religions, especially pagan ones, are capable of assimilating beliefs, rites and practices from each other, [2] and these three traditions probably intermingled and modified each other over the course of years in the ordinary way. But clearly the result was not homogeneous; legionary centres like York were more open to Roman influence, [3] while frontier stations on Hadrian's Wall manned by less Romanized provincials, together with ports such as London, inhabited by foreign traders, were more susceptible to the religions of the Orient. [4] Celtic beliefs are likely to have prevailed in country districts (though not in villas) and beyond the frontiers. [5] So much can be said from an archaeological study of cult sites, temples, and inscriptions.

But the evidence for the beliefs that lay behind these outward signs of worship is mainly found in inscriptions and literature. For the Roman and Oriental traditions these sources are satisfactory enough and the ground has been covered and covered again. [6] For the Celtic tradition the situation is much complicated by a complete lack of Celtic literature before the 5th century [7] and by a general paucity of classical literature on Roman Britain. Consequently we have to rely first on classical authors writing before the conquest or early in the Empire, like Caesar, Diodorus Siculus, Lucan, and Pliny, whose views on the Celts, though often accurate tended either towards romance or towards denigration and, secondly, on post-Conquest literature (like the *Mabinogion*) from Ireland, Scotland and Wales, which was often not written down until the Middle Ages. Two fundamental criticisms of the use of such sources immediately come to mind. First, they do not deal with the period in question, and secondly, they cover a far wider range of territory than Roman Britain. It is, of course, accepted that in matters of detail there is no precision, but the archaeological evidence throughout North-West Europe for the temporal range of the Celtic cult of the head, from before Roman times, through the Roman occupation, and into the post-Roman period, backing up the evidence of both the early and the late literature, [8] allows us to use this literature to make some general comments on Celtic beliefs under the Roman occupation. On certain matters with which we are particularly concerned, such as the immortality of the soul, the general agreement between the early classical writers and the post-Roman sources is most important. [9] In addition, the wide geographical range of certain types of Celtic iconography and architecture like the horned god and the square porticoed temple make it legitimate on occasions to draw parallels between, for instance, northern Gaul and southern Britain. [10] Naturally all this evidence

has to be used with care, but the information it is capable of giving on Celtic beliefs is far superior to any information that can be culled for earlier periods or for farther-flung regions.

A criticism which is possibly more severe is aimed at the sources of information for all these traditions, namely, that they describe either aristocratic religious ideas or the common people's beliefs from a biased aristocratic point of view. It is true that for the Mediterranean traditions it is usually possible to make cautious inferences from epitaphs about the ordinary religious beliefs concerned with the Afterlife. But for the Celtic tradition the early classical and later medieval sources have a distinct aristocratic flavour. [11] On the other hand, it is likely that the Romans with their emphasis on peace rather than war and urban rather than rural development [12] would have levelled society out so that the old aristocratic beliefs would have spread more evenly. But caution is needed; it may well be on this very point that evidence is provided by the cemeteries themselves. [13]

Of the three traditions, clearly the Roman occupies the pivotal position, both as the official tradition of the conquering legions and as the intermediary between the Oriental and Celtic traditions. Obviously, by itself it covered a wide range of beliefs, where even in Italy Etruscan ideas differed from Samnite, but such was the unifying force inherent in the army and civilian government that the central Roman thread of belief must be considered the most important. This Roman tradition had certain superficial similarities to the Celtic tradition. An example of this can be seen in the divine founder of the Roman race, Mars himself, who had a wide range of responsibilities, including success in war and in peace, health, and fertility. [14] These made him a tribal patron typical of the Celtic gods, who were similarly all-rounders in excellence, [15] whereas the normal classical gods had their functions more strictly limited. Mars was often to be found as one of a triad of gods with Jupiter and Quirinus in urban cults and with Janus and Jupiter in rural cults. [16] Celts, too, favoured triads with three-headed busts and three-horned animals being sculpted to represent deities. [17] Compared with the Greeks, the Romans were also closer to the Celts in being affected by the divinity of natural and agricultural features. The Fons Bandusiae, like Coventina's well near Hadrian's wall, received its annual sacrifice. [18] Even human sacrifice, a Celtic practice so abhorred by Rome, was found in Rome itself during the Punic wars. [19] The point is that Roman religion had a background which made possible a certain degree of assimilation to the Celtic and northern religions through the famous *'interpretatio Romana'* of Tacitus. [20]

Yet the very passage in which Tacitus uses this phrase puts one on one's guard against assuming that gods in Britain which have Roman forms or names are necessarily Roman in spirit. For the German gods, to whom Tacitus here refers and whom natives called Castor and Pollux, were clearly (because of their effeminate and professional priests) very different from the classical pair of the same name. Frere stresses the bewildering kaleidoscope of combinations which *interpretatio Romana* involved: a god whose cult statue was totally classical may have had an inscription to the Celtic Mars Lenus, or what looked like a Celtic deity may have had underneath it an inscription 'to Mars and the divinity of the Roman Emperor'.[21] One can only try to define the main differences between the Roman and Celtic traditions at the time of the Roman invasion of Britain in order to see what extremes existed in the beliefs which we are examining.

Roman religion was essentially timid and unimaginative. Ferguson draws an interesting contrast between the Greeks and the Romans: whereas the former uncovered their heads for prayer to expose themselves to divine influence, the latter covered theirs to avert evil omens.[22] Almost all Roman mythology was derived from Greece; there was little that was native—a situation which has a curious parallel in Italy today, where there is an almost total lack of folklore. The Romans were clearly frightened by the unknown, a fear which they overcame by an intense reliance on ritual. Each god, as we have seen, had his own special sphere of influence: the Romans were very careful to address the right god on the right occasion by the right name.[23] Even as late as the 5th century St Augustine thought it worthwhile attacking this procedure.[24] Where possible, elaborate rituals were conducted for the household or for the state by the appropriate authority of the *paterfamilias* or of the official.[25] If at any point a blunder was made, however, the whole procedure was repeated and an additional sacrifice was offered by way of atonement.[26] This cautious attitude towards the gods of the heavenly regions was even more pronounced when it was the gods of the underworld who were concerned. Most of them were 'unmentionable' (*nefandi*) or 'hated' (*invisi*)[27] and intercourse with them was limited to three days in August, October, and November, when the Mundus, a deep pit dug in the centre of each Latin town, was opened to receive libations.[28] Death was a fearsome state. The law of the Twelve Tables stated that no man was to be buried or burnt within a city.[29] When the dead bodies were put away there was a long ritual starting with the nearest relative's last kiss and finishing with the final opening of the dead man's eyes.[30] One of the reasons for Roman care in burial was fear of ghosts: a man without the minimum covering of earth at burial could haunt.[31] Consequently they had special festivals to placate the spirits of the dead: the Parentalia in February and the Lemuria in May.[32] Not surprisingly, in view of this desire to ward off anxiety, the Romans had few ideas of their own about an afterlife. During the 1st and 2nd centuries this is reflected in hundreds of tomb inscriptions all over the Empire of ordinary men and women,[33] where the most that is hoped for is that the earth should lie lightly on a vaguely animate corpse within the tomb. 'Let the earth lie lightly on you' (*Sit tibi terra levis*) is a constant refrain.[34] Perhaps there existed an ultimate fate too fearful to be contemplated in the eternal punishment against which Lucretius inveighed, and maybe it was in a mood of Epicurean relief that some tombs had inscribed 'We are mortal, not immortal' (*Sumus mortales, immortales non sumus*).[35] However, most tomb inscriptions left aside speculation and concentrated on the grief of the bereaved or on the past good work of the deceased.

It is incontrovertible, however, that a change of emphasis towards hope for an afterlife took place late in the 2nd century and during the 3rd century. For the ordinary man this possibly sprang from his desire to be remembered (evident in the 1st and 2nd centuries): where possible, tombs had been put close to roads leading out of towns so that inscriptions could be read.[36] 'Titus Lollius has been placed near the road so that passers-by may say "Hullo Lollius",' is a typical example and shows, too, that the *Manes* or departed spirits could be thought to exist in an amorphous state inside their tombs.[37] That they should not be disturbed was a constant care of the law,[38] and that they should receive burial at all became increasingly the care of funerary colleges, set up specially by and for lower members of society.[39] On the birthdays of the deceased or at the special festivals libations were poured to the dead, very often down pipes which led to the dead person's mouth, thus supplementing the rations which they were given in bowls and flagons when they were originally buried.[40] It was this vague and comparatively joyless belief in existence after life and this desire to be remembered that led the ordinary Roman to be interested in the more definite promises for future bliss held out by Oriental religions.

And so, when the Romans came into constant contact with the Celts it was the latter's definite belief in an afterlife which struck them most about their religion. They thought that the Celts believed in a sort of transmigration of souls, after the manner of Pythagoras. As Caesar says: 'The cardinal doctrine which they [the Druids] seek to teach is that souls do not die but after death pass from one to another.[41] One should not take the Pythagoreanism very seriously, but clearly the classical authors were impressed enough by the strange vividness of the Celtic beliefs before the period of the Roman domination to describe them and to stress that all possessions dear to the dead man, including on occasions, slaves, and dependants were burnt with him at his funeral for his enjoyment in the after-world.[42] What the exact rites were that went with these funerals we do not know. Probably they differed from one area to another, just as objects buried with dead people ranged from pottery to fire-dogs and from toilet sets to weapons.[43] But these probably reflect what was considered proper to have in an afterlife rather than anything more general about its nature. It is in the later literature that the nature of the afterlife is made more clear: when in the *Mabinogion* Bran the Blessed's severed head gave his seven followers a foretaste of it, it was a place of delight and wonder, reflecting the joys of the present world.[44] Now, the *Mabinogion*, like all other Celtic literature, is a product of that oral tradition which was stressed by the Druids even in Caesar's day. Herein seems to lie a great difference between the Celtic and Roman traditions. The Celtic tradition seems to have had its own myths and legends which it constantly elaborated with an invention totally alien to the Roman. Like the Greeks the Celts had no basic dread of describing what the Romans would have deemed 'unmentionable'. In the legends there was a concourse between the human and divine: goddesses could turn themselves into ravens and back again with bewildering rapidity, Morrigans became hags, and magic swine poured out of the gates of the afterlife.[45] No wonder that the classical writers thought that the Druids believed in the transmigration of souls!

The archaeological evidence over a period of time seems to back up the picture given by the literary sources of the relationship between the divine, the dead and the living. The 3rd century BC enclosures at Libenice (Czechoslovakia) and the ritual shafts at Holzhausen and Vendée show a definite connection between religious site, chthonic sacrifice, and burial.[46] Later there sprang up in Celtic lands under the Roman occupation important temples associated with cemeteries, like Sanxay, Le Donon, and Bac des Curs in France and Lancing in Britain. Indeed, Lewis is of the opinion that worship of the dead was one of the roots from which the Roman-Celtic temple grew.[47]

What is certainly clear is that Celtic religion included amongst its more popular powers deities who controlled death, amongst other things, like Cernunnos and Epona.[48] These deities were certainly not 'unmentionable'. Far less was Dis Pater, as Caesar called the ancestor of the gods, although as he caused the Celts to count dates by nights and not by days he was also a lord of the underworld.[49] This combination of chthonic and heavenly functions was easy for a Celtic tribal god, and is yet another sign of a more direct and personal relationship between men and gods in the matter of death. The Romans, however, dismissed it as superstition and bad.[50] Perhaps they were right; human sacrifice is likely to occur where the distinctions between life and death are blurred.[51]

Such then may have been the essential differences in the beliefs of the Celtic and Roman religions when they met in Britain in the 1st century AD. What happened then seems very difficult to trace because of the paucity of evidence. This is partly due to a strange lack of burials just prior to the Roman invasion. It is not clear how the Celts of that age in many areas buried their dead,[52] and therefore there is no real yardstick by which to gauge the burials found thereafter. What is more, only a very small percentage indeed of the burials in the earliest part of the Roman occupation have been found. The fact, then, that most known burials exhibit Roman traits in their tomb inscriptions[53] means little more than that they contain soldiers or a few natives who have been Romanized close to the main Roman centres. However, it is certainly likely that natives who have been encouraged by a conqueror to abandon an essentially agricultural and warlike way of life[54] will have changed their views about the afterlife to some extent, and will have accepted at least the material aspects of the conquering religion, the tombs and the grave furniture. But this does not necessarily mean to say that they will have abandoned a vivid idea of an afterlife, even if this idea has changed because its model in the life of the living has changed. Certainly the marked presence of mainly Celtic deities with or without *interpretatio Romana* and the special Romano-Celtic temple which sprang up in southern Britain (and in northern Gaul and Germany as well) during the Roman occupation seem to indicate that throughout the first four centuries after Christ Celtic ideas were strong.

Religion, though conservative, does not remain static, however. At the very time of Claudius's conquest of Britain, powerful religious forces from the East with beliefs about the afterlife were entering Rome. It was Claudius himself who gave sanction to the more extravagant rites of Cybele from Asia Minor which had been repressed since the goddess's entry into Rome in 213 BC.[55] Cumont thinks that he did this to counteract the influence of another Eastern Cult, that of Egyptian Isis which a few years previously had been allowed to enter Rome by Caligula.[56] At all events, Eastern religion exercised a growing influence until it reached its highest point in the 3rd century. Apuleius, a convert to Isis, wrote about his experience in the middle of the 2nd century. Not much later, Jupiter Dolichenus, a deity from Commagene, popular with the army, was to be found in Britain. Persian Mithras, another divine object of military enthusiasm, had shrines in London and along Hadrian's Wall during the 3rd century AD, while Cybele and Isis were also to be found on the Wall and in London, though their temples have not been

discovered.[57] What was important about most of these Oriental cults is that without destroying the structure of Roman religion they offered to their initiates a purer life and (what particularly concerns us) the hope of victory over death.[58] But to be initiated was not easy. To enter the cult of Mithras, the initiate, who had to be male, underwent various ordeals. The devotees of Isis needed riches.[59] In fact, generally speaking, proselytes of these mystery religions were from the more wealthy strata of society. Once initiated, the devotee was helped by the god himself to reach immortality. Hermes tells Julian 'keep Mithras's commandments, preparing an anchorage and safe harbourage for yourself, and when you have to go hence, you will do so with a good hope and have god as a kindly leader for yourself'.[60] Essentially, the ritual for passing the gates of death were performed on initiation rather than at the deathbed. As Lucius says in *The Metamorphoses*, 'At midnight I saw the sun shining as if it were noon: I entered the presence of the gods of the underworld and the gods of the upper world. I stood near and worshipped them'.[61] This being so, we should not necessarily expect to find a distinct burial rite for initiates.

Initiates were, however, not the only ones affected by the mystery religions. Clearly these religions had a powerful visual appeal in their public ceremonies. Their music was strident, their dances were extravagant. Onlookers, without ever expecting to become initiates, must have shared some of their hopes through a personal, informal devotion.[62] Certainly with the rise of these religions there occurs increasing emphasis (depicted in sarcophagi and elsewhere) on the expectation and hope of an afterlife.[63] Many, too, have seen the move away from cremation to inhumation as the result of greater respect for the body which was about to have a new life.[64] These hopes were not often expressed by pictures of the Oriental mysteries themselves, but more by the symbolic use of classical motifs, in particular of the legends surrounding Dionysus, the god of fertility. Notable examples of this are the nine 2nd century sarcophagi of the Roman family of Calpurnii Pisones, on which the most common sculpted picture is Dionysus's rescue of Ariadne, symbolizing the rescue of the buried man from death.[65] Elsewhere, there are scenes of vintage, symbolizing happiness in the world beyond, or of seaborne deities, depicting the journey to the Isles of the Blest,[66] a Greek afterworld which begins to receive recognition early on at the beginning of the Empire.[67] Yet sarcophagi such as these, where the hopes of the dead person or his relatives are obvious enough, by their very nature belong to rich people. How the poor expressed their hope for a future life—if they did so at all— is less clear. A statuette of Cybele was found in an undecorated coffin at Neuss and a bronze figure of Isis in a coffin at Noyelles-sur-Mer,[68] but by *interpretatio Romana* these statuettes might have stood for Celtic goddesses.

In Britain, apart from the evidence already quoted for the presence of mystery religions,[69] their more general influence can be seen as early as the 3rd century amongst the better-off, one of whose children had a lead coffin decorated with scallop shells and Bacchic figures alluding to the journey to the Isles of the Blest.[70] It can also be seen in the 4th century mosaics in villas of the rich in certain areas of southern Britain, where the eschatological symbolism of personified seasons, dolphins, Orphei, Bacchi, Bellerophons, and Christian Chi-Rhos jostles with literary and mythological scenes.[71]

Such, then, is an attempted reconstruction of the general background of pagan religious attitudes to be found in

Roman Britain. Within this framework each area is likely to display different features of an endemic kind and lean towards one or other of the traditions. Over the course of three centuries there were clearly changes. On the whole it is likely that the negative attitude of the Roman tradition towards the afterlife was eroded, with the Oriental trends strengthening the native tradition. What is clear is that the Oriental trends did not take over completely from the native: the popularity of Celtic temples, for instance, at Lydney, Maiden Castle, and Woodeaton, in the second half of the 4th century is proof of that.[72] In fact, compared with Gaul,[73] Britain received comparatively little of the direct Oriental tradition, a circumstance which could be due either to her peripheral position or the strength of her own native cults which fulfilled the same desires. The two alternative reasons are really just the two sides of one coin, for the further west a province was from Rome and foreign influence, the more likely was it that its religion was personal and positive.

References

1   See the forthcoming publication of G N Clarke's *The Roman Cemetery at Lankhills* in M Biddle (ed) *Winchester Studies 3*, (2) (Oxford: Clarendon). All the material relating to this cemetery and its religious practices will be treated in this publication
2   e.g. Cumont, F (1922) *The After Life in Roman Paganism, passim*
3   Frere, S (1967) *Britannia*, 195 (London: Routledge)
4   Lewis, M J T (1966) *Temples in Roman Britain*, 99ff (Cambridge: CUP)
5   Frere 1967, 313. If the native tongue was the main language of the countryside as opposed to the towns, one must imagine that without the impact of a missionary religion like Christianity the inhabitants of the countryside would have kept their basic beliefs.
6   Cumont, F (1922) *The After Life in Roman Paganism* (New Haven)
    Cumont, F (1949) *Lux Perpetua* (Paris)
    Cumont, F (1929) *Les réligions orientales dans le paganisme romaine* (Paris)
    Richmond, I A (1950) *Archaeology and the After Life* (University of Durham/OUP)
    Nock, A D (1933) *Conversion* (London: OUP)
    Ross, Anne (1967) *Pagan Celtic Britain* (London: Routledge)
    Piggott, S (1968) *The Druids* (London: Thames and Hudson)
7   Ross 1967, 3
8   Ross 1967, 61-126
9   e.g. Lucan *Pharsalia* I, 456; cf Hyde, D (1967) *A Literary History of Ireland*, 94-104 (London: Benn)
10 Ross 1967, 127ff; Lewis 1966, 99ff
11 e.g. Caesar *de Bello Gallico* VI, 13; *The Mabinogion, Pwyll, Prince of Dyfed*, 3 (London: Everyman)
12 Tacitus *Agric.* 21
13 In particular, see note 1 above
14 Rose, H J (1948) *Ancient Roman Religion*
15 Ross, A (1970) *Everyday Life of the Pagan Celts*, 159
16 Rose 1948, 62
17 For Britain, Ross 1967, 74; for northern Gaul, Brogan, O (1953) *Roman Gaul*, 187 (London: Bell)
18 Horace *Odes* III, 13; Lewis 1966, 88. See also Pliny, *Epistles* VIII, 8 for the Italian temple complex at the springs of Clitumnus, which in its setting, extravagance, and purpose would have done credit to any 'Celtic' shrine, like Springhead (Kent), based on such a natural feature
19 Livy XXII, 57
20 Tacitus *Germ.* 43
21 Frere 1967, 326
22 Ferguson, J (1970) *The Religions of the Roman Empire* 99
23 e.g. Catullus XXXIV, 21-2
24 St Augustine *Civitas Dei* IV, 22
25 Cato Maior *de Agri Cultura* 143; CIL II, 5439
26 Ogilvy, R M (1969) *The Romans and their Gods* 25
27 Ogilvy 1969, 25; Vergil *Aen.* VIII, 245
28 Warde Fowler, W (1910) *The Roman Festivals* 211
29 Cicero *de leg* II, 23
30 Toynbee, J M C (1971) *Death and Burial in the Roman World* 43ff (London: Thames and Hudson)
31 Horace *Odes* I, 28
32 Toynbee 1971, 63ff
33 Dill, S (1904) *Roman Society from Nero to Marcus Aurelius*, 257ff. There is a good selection of inscriptions quoted here
34 For Britain, CIL VII, 540, 743, 1014; for Latium (e.g.) CIL XIV, 1001, 1125, 2822
35 CIL XI, 856
36 Dill 1904
37 ILS 4745
38 de Visscher, F (1963) *Les droits des tombeaux romains*
39 Dill 1904, 259ff. But, as Dill points out, it would be a mistake to think that these funeral colleges catered only, or even mainly, for the burial of their members
40 Toynbee 1971, 51ff
41 Caesar *de Bello Gallico* VI, 14; Diodorus Siculus V, 28; Lucan *Pharsalia* I, 450-8
42 Caesar *de Bello Gallico* VI, 19
43 Biddle, M (1967) 'Two Flavian burials from Grange Road, Winchester' *Antiq. J.* **47**, 224-50
44 *Mabinogion* 38ff
45 e.g. Ross 1967, 244f
46 Piggott 1968, 72ff
47 Lewis 1966, 6; van Doorselaer, A (1967), *Les Nécropoles d'Epoque Romaine en Gaule Septentrionale* (Dissertationes Archaeologicae Gandenses **10**), 216f
48 Ross 1967, 149
49 Caesar *de Bello Gallico* VI, 18
50 Pliny *Nat. Hist.* XXX, 13
51 For a discussion on human sacrifice see chapter on religion by the present author in Clarke forthcoming
52 Ellison, A, and Drewett, P (1971) 'Pits and potholes in the British Early Iron Age' *Proc. Prehist. Soc.* **37**(1), 190ff
53 e.g. CIL VII, 92, 205, 245, 478
54 Tacitus, *Agric.* 21
55 Cumont 1929, 83
56 Cumont 1929, 84
57 Richmond, I A (1954) *Roman Britain* 208-12 (Penguin)
58 Apuleius *Metamorphoses* XI, 4
59 Apuleius *Metamorphoses* XI, 22
60 Julian *The Caesars* 336C
61 Apuleius *Metamorphoses* XI, 23
62 Cumont 1929, 67
63 Richmond 1950, 27ff
64 Richmond 1950, 19
65 Richmond 1950, 30ff
66 Ferguson 1970, 145
67 Ashmole, B (1967) 'A new interpretation of the Portland vase' *J. Hellenic Stud.* **87**, 1
68 van Doorselaer 1967, 76, 119
69 cf Note 57 above
70 Toynbee, J M C (1962) *Art in Roman Britain* 179ff (London: Phaidon)
71 Smith, D J (1969) 'The mosaic pavements' in Rivet, A L F (ed) *The Roman Villa in Britain* 82ff (London: Routledge)
72 Frend, W H C (1968) 'The Christianisation of Roman Britain' in Barley, M W, and Hanson, R P C (eds) *Christianity in Britain 300-700*, 39 (Leicester: University Press)
73 Hatt, J-J (1970) *Celts and Gallo-Romans*, 276

Germanic burials in the Roman Iron Age

Malcolm Todd

When the archaeologist studies the burials of a culture, he is dealing with the observable remains of the last rites which society thought fit to perform on behalf of its departed members. Before turning to a brief survey[1] of the main burial forms adopted by the Germanic peoples outside the Roman Empire, it therefore seems proper to sketch an outline of Germanic society in so far as the largely Roman written sources allow. When the structure of Germanic society is first clearly revealed to us about AD 100 in the *Germania* of Tacitus, like most barbarian societies it is seen to be based upon the family unit and groups of interconnected families or kindreds.[2] Most people in a tribe, or *civitas,* were men of free birth and these men formed a tribal assembly which took major decisions regarding peace and war, judged the more serious criminal cases, and filled certain elective offices. Over the free men was a class (category might be a less misleading term) of more prominent individuals whom Tacitus calls *principes.* A place among these *principes* was earned only by those who could claim noble birth or whose fathers had performed outstanding services. From their ranks were chosen military chieftains, kings, and most probably priests. They also formed a council which discussed matters affecting the whole tribe, and could thus exert considerable influence over all the people. The retinues of kings and war-leaders were also drawn from among the ranks of the *principes,* but whether or not, or to what extent, they constituted a sharply defined class is still a matter of debate. In early Germanic society as a whole, however, there is little evidence of rigid class divisions and thus of the strife which these often engender. But it is obvious that in a society geared to warfare, certain individuals and families would have means and opportunities of acquiring more wealth, and thus a higher social position, than others. Social differentiation does not seem to have been marked in the pre-Roman Iron Age in Germania, but the arrival of the Romans on the Rhine and the Danube stimulated many changes in the relations between different levels in barbarian society, particularly in its upper echelon.

It is against this background that early Germanic cemeteries must be studied. We would expect the impact of Rome to have left some mark on the pattern of burial, as it did on the fabric of society, at an early date: and so it does. Before pursuing the matter further we must review the general character of Germanic burials in the earlier Roman Iron Age.

The general pattern of burial

Of the hundreds of thousands of recorded burials which date from the period between 100 BC and AD 300, the great mass are cremations, a rite which became the norm in northern Europe in the Middle Bronze Age and remained dominant throughout the pre-Roman Iron Age. Towards the end of the pre-Roman period, i.e. the later decades of the 1st century BC, occasional inhumations are found in the Germanic territories, these being usually interpreted as representing intruders from the south or the east. During the first two centuries AD, inhumation was practised alongside cremation in several areas, notably in Denmark, Pomerania, and the lower Vistula valley, and most commonly in North Jutland and southern Sweden. There is evidence, too, that over much of central and eastern Germania, inhumation was seen as the appropriate form of burial for members of the highest level in society, as we will see. From the 3rd century onward, inhumation became relatively common in certain regions, especially in the south, and was everywhere practised with greater frequency. Areas where it was particularly common include Bohemia and Moravia, Thuringia, parts of Silesia, the upper Oder valley, and those parts of Rumania which formed the Roman province of Dacia until the 270s. Roman influence is often invoked to explain this spread of inhumation, but it should not be overlooked that the nomadic peoples of south-eastern Europe were also inhumers, though little is known about their cultural contacts with the Germanic peoples.

Despite their wide geographical spread, these inhumations share several common features. The great majority are aligned north-south, although the head of the corpse might be to either direction. Generally, the grave-pit is wide and deep, considerably more so than those provided for burials in the Roman provinces. The grave-goods were usually laid out with some care, frequently in the same general arrangement. The much commoner cremations display a greater degree of variety, though very few give the impression of being carelessly thrust into the ground. Surface marking of cremations, apart from barrows and cairns, seems to have been rare. Very occasionally, square settings of stones are recorded around small groups of burials, more commonly square ditched enclosures, the latter probably a regional phenomenon of western Germania. Barrows and standing monoliths are not uncommon in the lower Vistula region, barrows and cairns in Denmark, southern Sweden, and the Baltic islands of Oland, Gotland, and Bornholm. Occasionally, 'cenotaphs' are encountered, in the form either of empty pits amid graves, or of pits containing pottery and other goods but no cremated bone or other skeletal remains. The burials of children are represented by disproportionately few instances in almost all cemeteries, while those of babies are rarely represented at all. At Tišice in Bohemia, for example, out of 104 bodies, only nine were those of children less than 15 years of age, and none of these were infants. In some cases it may be that social rank was a factor in determining where a child should be interred, since some child-burials are accompanied by rich grave-goods not unlike those appropriate to their father or mother. Such a case was the boy burial from Bornitz, which contained two spurs, a belt, two knives, a drinking-horn, and silver dress-ornaments.

British excavators, more familiar with Anglo-Saxon cremations in the Elbe-Weser regions than with burials in other areas, are prone to think of cremations as very monotonous in their character and the arrangement of their goods. In fact, there are several different kinds of early Germanic cremation. The three major forms are distinguished by German archaeologists by the names

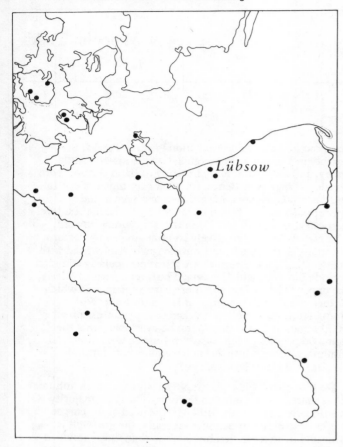

1   Fürstengräber of the Lübsow group: 1st-2nd centuries

Urnengrab, Brandgrube, and *Brandschüttungsgrab.* The commonest form is the *Urnengrab,* in which the cremated remains have been carefully collected up and placed in a pot, metal vessel, or occasionally a wooden, leather, or cloth container. The *Brandgrube* contains the cremated remains along with burnt material from the pyre, the *Brandschüttungsgrab* the same but including also broken or burnt grave-goods, usually pottery. Various other rites of cremation are attested, but none is particularly common. One of the most striking is represented in a number of cremation cemeteries (termed the Dobrodzién type) in one localized area of southern Poland, in which the remains of different bodies were not kept separate but spread, together with the grave goods, in a layer of ash and bone across the whole site.

Male and female cemeteries

In the lower Elbe basin from Holstein to central Germany numerous cemeteries of the earlier Roman Iron Age contain either exclusively male or exclusively female burials.[3] This phenomenon has long been recognized and there seem to be no grounds for the doubts expressed about its reality in recent years. The cemeteries of male burials include a high proportion of graves without goods, alongside a considerable minority which contain weapons and other warrior equipment, bronze buckets and basins, usually Roman imports. In the female cemeteries, a large number of burials contain ornaments and sometimes implements appropriate to a female *milieu:* such things

as weapons and belt-parts are absent. In some cemeteries it is very likely that men and women were buried in different areas and in these cemeteries there is a little evidence that cremation-urns of different types were used for the two sexes.

What lies behind this practice is uncertain. Religious grounds have commonly been invoked—and this may very well be correct. But another possible explanation is that the male cemeteries represent formal bands of warriors, or even retinues, and those of women their female dependants. Whatever the actual significance of these cemeteries, their existence clearly casts doubt on the social importance of the clan or kindred, at least in this region of Germania. The custom of segregated burial survived longest in Holstein and the Altmark, lingering there until the late Roman period. Elsewhere, it seems to have died out during the 2nd and early 3rd century.

Fürstengräber of the Roman Iron Age

Graves of the early Roman Iron Age which contain outstandingly rich goods are by no means common. The first clear differentiation between the graves of rich or otherwise distinguished individuals and run-of-the-mill burials occurs in the 1st century BC. A small number of cemeteries in the regions about the western Baltic shores contain the occasional rich burial, a recently recorded instance being the cart-burial at Husby (Kreis Flensburg). The date is significant. At this time, large areas of fertile, heavier soil were being opened up to agriculture in Jutland, Schleswig-Holstein, the Danish islands, and Mecklenburg, conditions in which individuals might gain relatively rapid access to wealth and social prestige. During the Roman Iron Age, several groups of *Fürstengräber* may be defined, and one series in particular, dating from the 1st and early 2nd centuries, is of outstanding interest.[4] This is the so-called Lübsow group, named after a site near Stettin in Pomerania where no less than five rich burials have been found. These burials of the Lübsow type occur either singly or in small groups, never in cemeteries, and the dead were normally inhumed. They are distributed from Bohemia to southern Norway, and from the Elbe valley to the Vistula; in other words they cover the heartlands of the Germanic tribes (Fig. 1). If the distribution map is to be trusted, there is something approaching a concentration of them about the western Baltic shores. The two examples in Bohemia (Repov and Zliw) and the sole instance on the lower Vistula (Rondsen) seem to be outliers. Significantly, none have been recorded from the Rhine-Weser regions, entered by Germanic groups late in the pre-Roman Iron Age.

The wealth of the equipment found in these graves elevates them far above the common run of early Roman Iron Age burials. Imports from the Roman world are very much to the fore, notably splendid banqueting services of bronze, silver, and glass vessels. Bronze wine-buckets, silver drinking-cups, and delicate glassware all testify to the wealth of these chieftains and their desire for the best apparatus for their feasts. One of the earliest of these *Fürstengräber,* if not the earliest of all, is the best known, that at Hoby on the island of Laaland. The Hoby grave-goods constitute the most astonishing collection of Greco-Roman metal vessels ever recovered from a grave in northern Europe. Those vessels comprised a pair of silver cups with decoration in relief representing, in one case, the meeting between Priam and Achilles and, in the other, the legend of Philoctetes; a plain silver cup to which a bronze handle had been fitted; a bronze tray and, also in bronze, a bucket, a patera, a jug, and two bronze-mounted drinking-horns. These objects provide us with a date of about the time of the birth of Christ for this grave. The items of native manufacture, though modest by comparison, are not negligible: seven bronze and silver brooches, two gold finger-rings, a bronze belt-buckle, a bronze knife, a bone pin, and three pottery vessels.

The largest concentration of such burials in one place is at Lübsow itself. Four burials, including one which had been plundered in antiquity, lay together at the Sandberg. The three which could be dated belonged to the 1st century AD. Two further richly furnished graves, accompanied by humbler interments, were found at Tunnehult, 3 km away, these dating from the 2nd century. The entire group thus spans the earlier Roman Iron Age.

The distinguishing marks of these graves of the Lübsow type may be summarized thus:

i   **The great majority, 29 or 30 out of 32, are inhumations,** in a period when cremation was in all regions of Germania the commoner rite.

ii   Special treatment of the burial site has frequently been recorded. Cairns or barrows were in some cases erected and the bodies were usually enclosed in either wooden coffins or stone-lined chambers.

iii A significant proportion of the grave-goods are imports of high quality. There is also marked homogeneity about the goods from the various graves.

These remarkable similarities between the 32 graves should be explained not as the result of the spread of some tribal or confederate burial rite but as a social phenomenon. In the Lübsow group we gain a rare, perhaps unique, glimpse of shared customs in the upper reaches of Germanic society, fostered no doubt by diplomatic contact and by intermarriage between the leading families of different tribes.[5] These chieftains and their womenfolk had risen to prominence relatively recently and their families commemorated their wealth and social position by these elaborate funerals. Wheeler wrote of the Lübsow group 'It was as though now, with the advent of new resources under the Early Empire, the 'new rich' were reviving the magnificence of their own remote past. There is nothing to suggest the arrival of a new aristocracy from without: no known tribal or national boundary defines the revolutionary mode. An inter-tribal fashion, based upon an access of wealth, had swept across central Europe in front of the organised and masterful approach of the culture of the Mediterranean'.[6]

We might now add that the 'new rich' were not all that new and that they owed their 'access of wealth' to the opening up to agriculture of rich tracts of land in northern and central Germania.[7]

Richly furnished graves of the late 2nd and 3rd centuries are rare in all parts of Germania, but towards the end of the 3rd century another series of *Fürstengräber* is evident, **widely distributed but much less uniform than those of** the Lübsow group. These burials fall into a number of regional groups, the three most important being a group in Jutland and Mecklenburg, a group in the Elbe-Saale basin (including the well known graves at Leuna, Hassleben, and Voigstedt), and a group in Silesia and Slovakia (for example, Sackrau, Stráže, and Osztrópataka). Rich graves of this class are notably absent from Bohemia at this time, as they are from the Saxon territories about the lower Elbe and from the broad regions between the Rhine and the Weser.

The best recorded of these later Roman Iron Age graves

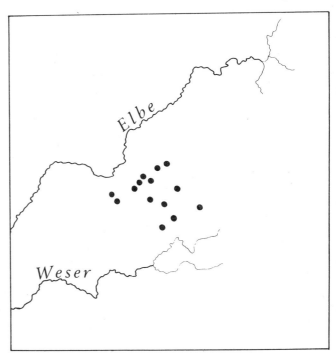

2   Elbe-Saale Fürstengräber: 3rd-4th centuries

are those in the Elbe-Saale basin[8] (Fig. 2). All are **inhumations, normally aligned north-south and often** encased in wooden coffins or grave-chambers. Male burials predominate. Among the splendid grave-goods Roman imports stand out, especially the bronze pans, bowls, and dishes and the glassware. The Germanic contribution is clearest in the silver brooches, gold rings and fine textiles. A peculiar feature is the common appearance of silver or bronze arrow-heads, always in threes, presumably a mark of rank. All the known graves date from the relatively limited period 270-310 and this circumstance, together with the fact that the Roman objects are mostly paralleled in contemporary Roman forts on the Danube frontier 100 miles to the south, suggested to Werner that the imported items had found their way northwards as loot. This is not, however, the only possible explanation. Some of this material, possibly most of it, may represent diplomatic exchanges rather than hostile contact. Certainly, some of the objects from Leuna and Hassleben in particular seem to fit more easily into a diplomatic scene than against a background of raids and looting, unless we suppose that these Elbe-Saale Germans were decidedly selective about what they looted. For there is a distinct tendency for the same kinds of object to occur in most of the burials. *Aurei* (but not apparently silver or bronze coins) are frequently found, either singly or in small numbers, in some cases in the mouth of the deceased, in others as parts of a necklace. Gold finger-rings with settings of Roman gems are also fairly prominent. Most telling, perhaps, is the presence of two heavy crossbow brooches at Leuna, one of them (in grave 2) a fine gilded silver specimen with niello decoration. Brooches of this kind were much favoured by Roman officers and others in the Imperial service from the later 3rd century onward. Objects like this could make significant as well as fine gifts to barbarian leaders, conferring status on the recipients as well as enriching them in a way which they would fully appreciate.

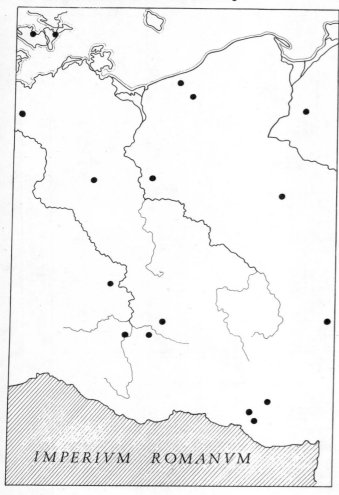

IMPERIVM   ROMANVM

*3   Distribution of graves containing combination of bowl and jug
(after H U Nuber)*

Certain of the Slovakian burials also contain objects of
remarkable quality which are difficult to explain as loot.
This is particularly true of the Roman objects from a
number of burials at Stráže, near Piestany in the Váh
valley.[9] Some of this material was dispersed shortly after
its excavation in the early part of this century and has only
recently been re-assembled by Bedřich Svoboda. The Stráže
graves contained a marvellous series of silver and bronze
vessels and ornaments, including a superb 2nd century lanx
in gilded silver and several other pieces of fine silver plate.
This concentration of splendid goods in chieftains' graves
is so marked that we are bound to wonder how the
material was acquired. Looting seems unlikely, for the
kinds of object represented here would appear ludicrously
out of place in some rustic Germanic court unless they
held some meaning for their owner. And it may be stressed
that the objects, however acquired, have not been treated
as loot. No slashed, bent, or otherwise violated pieces were
found. Surely, if these distinctive objects were spoils of
war, they would not have been treasured and kept in their
original form? The position of Stráže seems to settle the
matter. It lies only 40 miles north of the Danube frontier on
a strategic route which followed the course of the Vah.
The chieftains who held sway there could not be overlooked
by the Pannonian commanders. The evidence of the Stráže
burials is that their co-operation was sought and probably
obtained.

Roman influence on Germanic burials

No one who studies the Roman Iron Age cultures of
northern Europe can fail to be impressed by the pervasive
influence of Roman goods and ideas. But when Roman
practices or modes in the burial rites of Germanic peoples
are being sought and evaluated, it is to be borne in mind
that although there are clear indications that the Roman
world did indeed impinge upon the Germanic in this,
as in several other spheres, we cannot assume that a certain
rite or custom meant the same thing to a German as it
did to a Roman provincial. Indeed, with their very different
backgrounds and mundane circumstances, it would
be very surprising if it did. We can, then, record the
manifestation of Roman influence in burial customs
without necessarily coming near to grasping their essential
significance to the barbarian mind.

The presence of Roman equipment in burials other than
the richly furnished instances already mentioned is a
familiar phenomenon which need occasion no surprise. We
need not, therefore, comment further on the considerable
quantities of Roman pottery, brooches and other bronzes,
tools, and weapons found in graves, beyond noting that in a
few instances rather specialized implements found their
way into Germanic graves as fit accompaniments of the
dead, as in the case of a set of surgical instruments found
in a late Roman Iron Age grave near Halle. Certain other
kinds of Roman equipment, however, certainly held
significance in the sphere of barbarian burial custom. Finds
of Roman drinking-sets are very occasionally recorded in
the graves of the higher social levels, though these
say more about the habits of Germanic leaders, and their
consorts, in life than about ceremonies surrounding their
funerals. More interesting is the apparent selection of
Roman bronze vessels, especially buckets and bowls, as
containers for cremation burials and as accessories for
inhumations. This is a practice most marked in the Elbe
basin and in the lands about the western Baltic. The graves
are much more commonly male than female, and it
therefore looks as though the provision of high-quality
Roman vessels may well have been thought appropriate
for men of high standing or rank. Combinations of shallow,
handled bowls or *trullei* and trefoil-mouthed jugs (*urcei*)
are too frequent to be dismissed as coincidences. Pairs
of these vessels are familiar enough in Roman provincial
graves, but it is surprising to find them so widely distributed
in Germania[10] (Fig. 3). How they were used there must
remain unknown. In the Roman world they appear to have
served as sets for the ritual washing of hands. The
significance of Roman coins in Germanic burials is equally
difficult to assess. In many cases they may be no more than
ornaments or amulets, but others have plainly gone into the
burials in imitation of Roman custom. Coins in the mouths
of Germanic inhumations of the later Roman Iron Age are
by no means rare, though no collection of all the known
instances seems to have been published. From time to
time, a piece of precious metal jewellery served as a
substitute.

We may end with the most familiar of Roman equipment
in Germanic graves, and equipment which represents not
the impact of Rome on the barbarians but *vice versa*.
North-western Germania has yielded numerous graves
containing belt-parts, principally buckles and mounts,
of kinds produced in Roman military workshops in the
Rhine and Danube frontier areas, along with weapons
which are frequently impossible to label either Roman or
Germanic. These graves date from the mid-4th century
onward, the latest examples seeming to belong to the
first two decades of the 5th century. Closely similar burials

have long been known from northern Gaul and the German frontiers. These have endured much in recent archaeological literature.[11] Several scholars have attempted to link them with the shadowy *laeti* of late Roman sources, but this seems unlikely. This is not the place to discuss the matter at length, although it is true that more study of the entire corpus of such burials is needful to act as a corrective to the many confident statements which have of late been made about them. In the writer's view, most of the burials are to be interpreted as those of Germanic officers who had served in the regular Roman army before returning to Germania with at least some of their equipment. If this view is correct (and there is still no reason for dogma in this regard), it is interesting that many of the graves lie in Anglo-Saxon areas in Schleswig-Holstein and about the lower Elbe, and not where we might expect them, in the **Frankish territories on the lower Rhine and in Westphalia.**

These striking warrior-graves in one sense mark the end of the Roman Iron Age in northern Europe and point forward to an ascendant *Germanentum*. After their heyday, traces of Romanity in Germania virtually disappear. A new age began, though not unmindful of long years of contact with Rome.

Notes and References

1 A brief survey cannot do justice to this immense subject. All that I attempted in my contribution to the Seminar was to draw attention to some of the salient features of early Germanic burials, to relate, where possible, the pattern of burial to the Germanic social order, and to outline some of the Roman influences at work in Germania.

2 The best discussion of early Germanic society in English is Thompson, E A (1965), *The Early Germans* (Oxford: Clarendon)

3 Most recently discussed by T Capelle, *Studien über elbgermanische Gräberfelder in der ausgehenden Latènezeit und der älteren römischen Kaiserzeit, Münstersche Beiträge zur Vor- und Frühgeschichte*, Hildesheim (1971), 111-16

4 *Präh Zeitschr* **34-5** (1949-50), 58-111

5 Interestingly, Tacitus's account suggests that kingship was a more potent force in the eastern and northern regions of Germania, the general area of the Lübsow burials

6 Wheeler, R E M (1954) *Rome Beyond the Imperial Frontiers*, 34

7 It is surely no coincidence that social differentiation can be detected in the layout of certain settlement-sites at about the same time: H Jankuhn, *Deutsche Agrargeschichte I. Vor- und Frühgeschichte vom Neolithikum bis zur Völkerwanderungszeit*, Stuttgart (1969)

8 In general, W Schulz in *Mannusbibliothek* **22** (1922); idem, *Leuna. Ein germanischer Bestattungsplatz der spätrömischen Kaiserzeit*, Berlin (1953) and *Das Fürstengrab und das Grabfeld von Hassleben, Römisch-Germanische Forschungen* **7,** Berlin and Leipzig (1933)

9 B Svoboda, *Neuerworbene römische Metallgefässe aus Straze bei Piestany, Arch Slovaca Fontes* **11** (1972). The lanx is conveniently published in *Journ Rom Stud*, 58 (1968), 124-5, pls. III-VI. In general V Ondrouch, *Bohate hroby z doby rimskej na Slovensku* (1957), Tab. 47

10 See now, H U Nuber, 'Kanne und Griffschale', *Ber Röm-Germ Komm* **53** (1972), 1-252

11 e.g. J Werner, *Bonner Jahrb* **158** (1958), 372ff; K Böhner, *JRGZM* **10** (1963), 139ff; H Roosens, *Die Kunde,* **18** (1967), 89ff; R Günther, *Helinium* **12** (1972), 268ff; idem, 'Germanische Laeten, Foederaten und Gentiles im nördlichen und nordöstlichen Gallien in der Spätantike', in H Grünert (ed.), *Römer und Germanen in Mitteleuropa* (1975), 225-34; H W Böhme, *Germanische Grabfunde des 4 bis 5 Jahrhunderts zwischen unterer Elbe und Loire, Münchner Beiträge zur Vor- und Frühgeschichte* **19** (Munich 1974)

Burial in Latin literature: two examples

Richard Reece

Most evidence on burial in the Roman world is bound to come from archaeology—from the burials themselves—but Latin literature gives two very good texts on burial which repay study.

The first example, from the early Empire, is section 71 of the *Satyricon* of Petronius; the second example, from the end of the Empire, is Letter XII in Book III of the letters of Sidonius Apollinaris. The moment during the banquet of Trimalchio at which the host grows maudlin and details all arrangements for his death, including the design of his tomb, is almost well enough known not to need discussion, but no account of Roman burial would be complete without it. The letter of Sidonius is far less well known, and, as far as I know, this is the first time that it has been pressed into archaeological service.

It is generally agreed that the aristocratic Petronius was creating, in the character of the freedman Trimalchio, a picture of wealthy vulgarity. Since the account is tendentious we cannot take individual facts as absolute truths, but, conversely, the satire would have no bite or humour if the general framework created were not fairly close to the mark. Perhaps the overall fault in the episode is just this public mention of plans for death and burial. Plans must have been laid, sums set aside in wills, inscriptions, couplets, and epitaphs thought out, plots of land bought in fashionable places, and similar preparations made by many people in Rome and neighbouring cities without inviting the charge of vulgarity. But the discreet person did all this in silence, and the subject was one which only the naïvest *nouveau riche* would brag about. There may also be a knock here against those 'would-be middle-class' who had to resort to showy tombs flanking the roads out of Roman cities—the Via Appia Antiqua *par excellence*. The aristocrat would be buried with little fuss in his family mausoleum, a respectable poor family might have a small family plot in an appropriate burial ground, a slave would be interred in the *columbarium* of the family which he had served. Perhaps only the vulgar new arrival needs to buy up part of the roadside in order to erect a monstrosity to the glory of his quickly forgotten life.

Petronius portrays Trimalchio as certain of the reasons for having a large ornamental tomb well inscribed—remembrance in various forms. 'It is wrong to look after the house in which you live and to neglect the house in which you must stay much longer.' The statue and the inscription are to be put up carefully by his friend Habinnas so that 'your kind acts may make me live after death'. A sundial is to be placed in the middle of the sculptured composition 'so that whoever looks at the time, whether he wants to or not, will see my name'. The composition of the sculptured scene with Trimalchio in his glory doling out coins from a bag surrounded by his prize gladiator, his merchant ships in full sail, his favourite boy, jars of wine, and his wife and her pet dog, and the inscription which could only have caused raucous laughter rather than moist-eyed reverence are not our business here, for they belong to individual monuments rather than to more general ideas of death and burial. Mention of Fortunata, the wife, does bring up one further

point, for she has the misfortune a little further on in the banquet (end of section 74) to annoy Trimalchio. He retaliates with a 'flash of lightning', uses his utmost severity, and cuts her out of the frieze on the tomb. His own reason for doing this is so that she shall not be around to nag him when he is dead. If there is any serious intent in the disastrous effect this news has on Fortunata, it might be that she could hope to survive in memory as the wife of Trimalchio—but removed from this station she will inevitably fall into complete obscurity. Alternatively it may be a storm in a tea-cup with no serious intent at all.

Finally there is the matter of the method of burial and the burial plot. This is dealt with briefly, for Trimalchio sees little capital to be made out of it. He will be cremated, and will be buried in the monument on a plot of land of frontage 100 feet, extending back from the road for 200 feet. The monument is only to occupy a small part of this space: the rest will be devoted to trees, for 'I would like all sorts of fruit growing round my ashes—and plenty of vines'.

When we move to the letter of Sidonius we move from the classical to the medieval, the pagan to the Christian, the freedman to the aristocrat, and, most important, from the individual tomb to the cemetery. Sidonius, the distinguished country gentleman with a villa estate, panegyrist to three emperors (one of them, Avitus, his father-in-law), Urban Prefect at Rome in 468, and Bishop of Clermont-Ferrand in central France from 469, writes about the near-desecration of the grave of his grandfather, who had been Praetorian Prefect of Gaul under Constantine III in 408 and the first of the family to be baptized a Christian.

The letter starts with Sidonius on his way to the 'urbam arvernam', now Clermont-Ferrand. His point of departure is not stated, but the simplest suggestion is that he was travelling from his estate at Avitacum, south of Clermont, up to the city on business which kept him there for some time. As he came to the brow of a hill he saw coffin bearers in the cemetery in which his grandfather had been buried. 'The surface of the ground had changed from green to black, fresh soil was visible on the grave', when he gave the horse its head and rushed to the spot. The workmen, taking time to decide between flight and sorting the matter out, were thus caught in the act, and summary justice was executed on them then and there. Either Sidonius had a retinue or the gravediggers realized their mistake, for they accepted a beating 'severe enough to satisfy the hurt feelings of the survivors and to ensure secure rest to the dead'.

We have here an almost unique description of a graveyard only recently disused. 'It had been full for many (several?) years of cremated ashes (*bustualibus favillis*) and of bodies (*cadaveribus*) so that there was no room for another grave'. It was not altogether the grave-diggers' fault that they were desecrating a grave, for 'the mound which is piled up on the buried had returned to its pristine flatness; by the weight of snow and the daily wear of pouring rain the heap had been flattened. This was why the bearers dared to desecrate the spot with funerial tools for they believed it to be free of bodies'. However, the damage has been done, a warning has been given, and, to prevent further mishaps Sidonius instructs his nephew, the recipient of the letter, to 'gather the scattered material up again ready to be capped by a worked stone slab'. He sends, at the end of the letter, a twenty-line verse to be carved on the marble, and gives careful instruction that the mason be watched so that there are no blunders for which Sidonius will inevitably be blamed.

This puts forward the main points of the letter. Before extracting the implications which clamour for recognition, it is necessary to give the warning that most of Sidonius's letters are literary set-pieces, and that some of them may well owe more to the reworking of a literary theme which had seized his imagination than to anything which had happened to him or which he needed to communicate. The obvious cause of this letter is the twenty-line epitaph which, without a setting, might well have been rather short and obscure, which polished gem might therefore have been omitted from the 'collected works'. However, since I have heard of no likely classical inspiration for this letter we might as well profit from its implications.

Firstly we seem to have the picture of a rural graveyard. The journey is more than just begun, and the letter, presumably written from Clermont, expects to find the nephew Secundus not too far from the graveyard to put repairs in motion. It is perhaps simplest to see this as a graveyard in the country, within reach of the estates of Sidonius and his nephew, serving the neighbouring families. There is no suggestion that it is a family preserve or even a specifically Christian burial place.

The graveyard has been filled with cremations and inhumations. A Christian aristocrat finds nothing remarkable here just as, in Book III, Letter III, he finds the heaping of dead Goths inside a building and firing it more acceptable than hasty and ineffectual burial. Unless there is a wide ranging historical view here, from the 2nd century when cremation was common, to the 5th when inhumation prevailed, we have a record of a cemetery in which cremation and inhumation were practised side by side. Without stretching the evidence unduly, this observation might well be taken as an indication of the settlement of Germanic peoples in the Auvergne in the early 5th century, and a further indication that they preserved their burial rite of cremation.

Sidonius's grandfather originally had no gravemarker or tombstone. Sidonius expected the grave to be respected and assumed that the gravemound would ensure this. He himself records that in something less than 40 years the mound had disappeared, and adds the astonishingly modern touch of giving the natural environmental agencies which he thinks are responsible. Thus in at least one man's view of one cemetery reburial on ground already occupied was sacrilege and the way in which later interments were to be organized was by taking note of pre-existing gravemounds. There is no suggestion that this is a Christian innovation; we may reasonably expect that events would have been very similar if Sidonius's great-grandfather—a pagan—had been at risk. This seems to be a simple matter of delicacy and good taste. Matters are set straight by punishing the offenders—as much for the scruples of the living as the repose of the dead.

The epitaph on the plain marble slab must have caused great trouble to the local stone-cutter; it may well be one of the longest inscriptions in Gaul in the mid-5th century. Sidonius expects mistakes, a matter which suggests that

such inscriptions were rare. However, he does describe the epitaph as tardy, which might be taken to imply that while a gravemarker and epitaph would not have been expected in about 415 they may have been more common by 460. This may well be pushing implication beyond a reasonable limit.

In these two texts we have two completely different views of death and burial. Trimalchio is worried about being remembered, which is perhaps the nearest he can come to a conception of life after death. Whatever is to happen to him he wants to be surrounded by signs of his life, his money, wine jars, fruit trees. Perhaps if he could not have himself sculpted with these things he might have made arrangements for a more modest show—some coins in a purse, a beaker of wine, and some fruit on a platter. This is the mentality of the Roman tomb and furnished grave. Sidonius, in a world shortly to crumble around him, though he is almost certainly ignorant of the fact, belongs in a group of people who have come to terms with death, can see something after, and who regard burial as the decent deposition of an unwanted body while the person begins a new life.

Trimalchio had as his proudest boast at the end of his epitaph that 'he never listened to any philosophers'. Taking the term in its widest sense, no one in the religious, moral, and social turbulence of the later 5th century could have equalled Trimalchio.

The significance of plaster burials for the recognition of Christian cemeteries

Christopher J S Green

From its earliest days Christianity was very much a religion concerned with death, burial, and the resurrection of the body in the manner of Christ Himself. Cemeteries, the dormitories of those awaiting the Second Coming, were important establishments, especially where they included the resting place of a martyr or Christian Father. The Christians, in death as in life, were exclusive, setting aside special plots for their use, and dictating the use of particular burial rites.

Such sites should, then, be relatively easy to identify, but in the first place the more important cemeteries often lie buried beneath later churches commemorating some eminent figure buried there, and secondly, where no such continuity exists, the physical remains are so simple as to escape notice. Plain mausolea and unostentatious burials were the rule; the marble coffins of Arles or Rome, for instance, were always exceptional, this very asceticism **condemning these cemeteries to an archaeological oblivion** not shared by their materialist pagan contemporaries. Where such cemeteries have been identified it has been entirely the result of literary, topographic, and epigraphic evidence, while the object of the excavation has been the special burials and the history of the church buildings. Few if any Christian cemeteries have been studied as entities, as major sources for the study of both the early Church and the population of the Roman Empire.

It is not intended here to review all the available evidence even for the Roman Empire but to describe a series of cemeteries in North Africa, Germany, and Britain which have a number of features in common, including the use of an unusual and distinctive burial rite, gypsum or **lime-packed inhumation.**[1] **This study arose from the** writer's work on one particular site in Britain and the opportunity is taken here to give a summary of the results of work on that site.

Before considering these sites, something should be said of the general character and origins of Christian burial customs and comparison made with the contemporary non-Christian practices. The origin of the Christian burial rite is quite clear and, as stated by Athanasius, is in the first place a following of Jewish custom hallowed by the example of Jesus (Athanasius, *Vita Antonii* 90, Migne **XXVI, 968). Tertullian likewise states that the Christian** custom of burial was for the body to be anointed with spices and to be deposited in a mausoleum or monument, as directed by Christ (Tertullian, *De Resurrectione Carnis*, CXXVII). This follows closely the most detailed Gospel account, in which it is stated that Christ's body was anointed with myrrh and aloes, and bound up in linen cloths before deposition in a tomb which had never previously been used (*John*, 19, 39-42).

Minucius Felix emphasizes the abhorrence for cremation but also states that incense and wreaths were forbidden (*Octavius* 11, 4, 12, 6.) The latter statement, however, probably refers to the conduct of the funeral service rather than the process of preparing the body for burial.

The Christian had every reason for preserving the body, for not only was the Resurrection seen in very literal terms but it was thought liable to occur at any time. In the 2nd and 3rd centuries Christian teachers such as Justin Martyr in Rome and Tertullian in Carthage were proposing a literal resurrection of the body at the time of Christ's second coming, an idea which, although less popular in the East, was long-lived in the West. The belief in a physical resurrection must have been recognized as particularly Christian by the middle of the 2nd century, in view of the authorities' treatment of the martyrs of Lyons in 177. The martyrs' bodies were denied burial, deliberately cremated, and scattered so that they would have no hope of resurrection (Eusebius, *Hist. Eccles.* 1, V, ch. 1, 61-63).

In other cases it is known that those destined for martyrdom made prior arrangements for their remains to be collected and accorded proper burial. In this connection the account of the martyrdom of St Tarachus is most revealing, for the judge is recorded as scornfully rejecting the condemned man's request that his body be collected for proper burial and specifically referring to embalmment as the mode of burial (*Putas quia mulierculae aliquae post mortem corpus tuum habent aromatibus vel unguentis condire?*) (*Acts S Tarachi* 7.)

The frequent depiction of Lazarus as a figure swathed in bandages is also a hint of a contemporary practice of mummification rather than an attempt at historical accuracy.

The account of John also mentions another feature of the Christian burial, that the body should be placed in a tomb or grave not previously occupied. Closely allied to this, but not based on the same biblical authority, was the belief that burials should not be disturbed or overlain by later interments, an idea again originating from a desire to preserve the body intact for a physical resurrection.

Equally important was the placing of a burial near to some holy person; proximity to such a figure was thought to guarantee salvation, the martyr or bishop interceding as a patron at the Judgment (Cabrol and Leclerq **5,** 45-50). This is illustrated by an inscription from Trier referring to the deceased deserving to be buried nearer the holy than in fact was possible, so many burials having already been placed round the spot (Gose 1958, No. 466). This must have been a potent factor in the growth of early cemeteries round the burial places of early church leaders, saints, and martyrs. This practice may also hint at the status of unidentified special graves which have become foci within these cemeteries.

Beliefs about the resurrection must also lie behind the custom of orienting Christian burials with head to west, a custom presumably originating in the Christian practice of facing east in prayer, which in turn, arises from the various allusions to the sun as a metaphor for God and the belief that at the resurrection Christ would appear from the East (*Matthew* 24, 27; Cabrol and Leclerq, **12,** 2666-9). Indeed, with Constantine these biblical references to the sun seem to have fostered his confusion of worship and Christianity, this process of syncretism culminating in his conversion as a Christian (Jones 1962, 101). No doubt the burial custom became firmly established at the same period.

The authority for denying use of gravegoods is not explicit. Certainly Christ was not provided with any material goods and the symbolic renunciation of earthly riches would accord with Christian ideals of asceticism. However, it seems clear from some burials in the Catacombs and from the burials of Maria, wife of Honorius, near Old St Peter's, that gravegoods were permitted in some female graves, but were intended as marks of respect to the dead rather than furnishings for their use in an afterlife (Toynbee 1968, 190-1).

Some idea of the actual character of the cemeteries can be gained from the few examples scientifically excavated, although these are mainly of late date and confined to the northern provinces. However, the Catacombs at Rome and the well preserved North African surface cemeteries are particularly important, since the epigraphic and literary evidence available for these sites illustrate their origins and organization.

The Rome cemeteries originated in the private burial plots of rich influential families in the city, families which had been converted at an early date and, as patrons, had provided meeting places and burial facilities for the community. Rich and poor were therefore brought together in death, the wealthy and church leaders differentiated by more elaborate burial monuments. These cemeteries were, in the first place, *areae* or surface cemeteries; it was only where space was limited and the subsoil suitable, as in the suburbs of Rome, that recourse was made to opening *coemeteria,* or underground burial places below the original graveyards.

Although the rich patrons at first owned and controlled cemeteries, the Church itself soon became involved, often acquiring the burial grounds by gift and then regulating their use and development. In the early 3rd century the catacomb of St Calixtus was established under the administration of the Church (Kirsch 1947, 15). In Africa, records of the Diocletianic persecution at Cirta make it clear that by the end of the 3rd century the Church organization there included grave diggers, presumably employed in a cemetery administered by the Church (Zwisa, 185-97).

Limited investigation of the surface cemeteries at Rome has shown them to consist largely of earth-dug graves with the bodies contained in amphora or tile tombs but whether they were generally oriented and denied gravegoods is unclear. Structures containing several bodies laid side by side, but separated by slabs of stone or low walls, are also known. The rich might lie in decorated coffins sited amongst the gardens that beautified the burial ground or were placed within mausolea or baldaquins (Testini 1966, 85-92). In the catacombs these features are reproduced by arranging the interments in rows along the passage walls and at intervals carving mausolea and baldaquins from the living rock. No attempt at orientation seems to have been made and would have been difficult to achieve but gravegoods, save the odd lamp, perfume flask, or item of jewellery, were excluded. Embalming was employed on occasions; more frequently the dead were swathed in a shroud surrounded by lime or plaster.

In the Rhineland cemeteries many of these features have been identified and, in addition, it has been shown that an attempt was made to lay out the dead in neat rows with head to west and to avoid disturbing previous interments; these sites will be further described below.

Christian attitudes towards death and burial are in marked contrast to those of the majority of the population. Without venturing too far into the vast topic of pagan burial customs, a few comparisons should, however, be drawn. Outside the Christian and Jewish faiths, burial rites rarely reflect any particular religious beliefs of the deceased. Amongst the most educated classes some denied the existence of any afterlife, others followed the classical conception of departed souls living in an underground Hades and Elysium, or in the Paradise across the ocean, the Isles of the Blest (Toynbee 1971, 33-9).

A few non-Christians followed an entirely secularized rite, simply treating burial as the tidy and respectful disposal of the discarded human frame. Belief in the underworld Paradise or the Isles of the Blest usually only influences the choice of designs on the stone or lead coffins, or in the tomb decorations of the rich, where Dionysiac or nautical scenes are often employed (Richmond 1950). Some saviour gods or mystery religions promised their adherents an afterlife of a vague and insubstantial nature, but the various initiation rites and ceremonies do not seem to have extended to matters of burial; mystic union with the god does not seem to have depended on the employment of particular burial methods (Nock 1932, 32ff). Burial clubs were indeed organized under the patronage of particular gods or goddesses, but it is clear that the main attractions were the social functions and the assurance that one would be buried in a decent fashion according to one's personal wishes (Toynbee 1971, 54-5; CIL, XIV, 2112). Municipal control of these clubs extended only as far as regulating the association of the living; the sole concern for the dead was to ensure that they were interred beyond the city boundaries. The only cemeteries owned and administered by the authorities might be those communal grave pits for paupers or the plots reserved for the more important municipal slaves.

Amongst the majority of the population in the Roman Empire the dead were clearly envisaged either dwelling in the grave or travelling to an underworld. In the case of the former, food, drink, clothing, and amusements were provided, or, as in the case of the Simpelveld coffin, the deceased was surrounded by representations of her material possessions (Espérandieu 1938, 107-8, No. 7795). The placing of lamps and shoes amongst gravegoods seems to refer to the idea of travelling to the underworld, just as the Charon's fee alludes to necessity to pay for one's transport across the Styx, and bird offerings refer to Mercury, the winged messenger who conducts the spirit to the afterlife.

Yet although the dead, as far as their means would allow, were placed to rest accompanied by material provision for a future existence, it seems that in many communal cemeteries in the northern provinces at least the plots were re-used over a period of years, perhaps for reasons of economy. The situation was complicated by the lack of any agreed alignment, and the plan often reveals a complicated sequence of burials overlapping and intersecting, aligned to any point of the compass (Lethbridge 1936, 109 ff; Wenham 1968, *passim*; Viner 1973, 195-200). The wealthiest, of course, could afford a private plot and a monument protecting the remains, often specifying its area and penalties for its desecration (Toynbee 1971, 73ff).

Cremation and inhumation were both practised, depending on personal preference, regional custom, and date. For the majority of the population regional burial traditions continued unaltered into the Roman period, the only change being the Romanization of grave-goods or funerary monuments. The only general tendency that can be observed is the gradual disappearance of cremation during the 2nd and 3rd centuries, a change which is usually ascribed to either a change in fashion or the growth of an undefined but widespread belief that inhumation might facilitate transition to an afterlife. Whatever the cause, it did not stem from the teaching of any pagan cult but might be a reflection of the spread of Christian beliefs (Toynbee 1971, 40). Embalming was sometimes employed for the wealthy but plaster-packed burials are not often encountered.

Following this outline of the differences in belief and practice between Christian and non-Christian, those cemeteries containing plaster burials must now be examined in greater detail. In plaster burials the body, wrapped in a shroud, was placed in a lead, stone, or wood coffin and then covered to some extent with a mass of the calcareous substance before the lid was set in place. Unfortunately most such burials, although exciting much attention at the time of their discovery, have not been scientifically examined, and it is often uncertain whether the material used was gypsum plaster or lime, or whether the packing was introduced to the coffin as a powder or mixed with water to form a slurry. In the case of some examples from Britain (see below), chemical analysis has confirmed that the packing was indeed gypsum, and in one case, where a full range of tests has been carried out, the gypsum had probably been used in the form of a hemi-hydrous powder (Green, forthcoming).

The purpose of the rite seems to be preservative, the dry powder being intended to prevent moisture reaching the corpse, or perhaps to absorb any liquid emanating from the body itself. The employment of lead for many of the coffins and the sealing of the lids on some stone coffins would support the former interpretation. Either gypsum powder or lime would be effective in this role; the former is absorbent and neutral, while the latter would vigorously soak up any liquid and produce a compound inhibiting bacterial action but, in the long term, destructive of human tissue. Allowing for the state of scientific knowledge at the time, however, it is fair to assume that both materials were used with the same end in mind. The packing material does not seem to have been used in isolation, the most important element in the rite was the embalming of the body itself. For this, less evidence is available but one burial in Britain from Dartford (Kent) still retained traces of aromatic gum, while another from Dorchester (Dorset) had a tarry substance coating the hair, still in place on the crown of the head (see below, 50). The rite did achieve some success, in that the hair has survived in some cases where the body was in a lead container. Whatever the long-term efficacy, gypsum burial, accompanied by embalming, does seem to have commended itself to at least some Christians as a burial rite that accorded with the best Christian traditions, and would be of practical assistance in the preservation of the body until the Resurrection.

The earliest instances of plaster burials are in fact of a non-Christian character and date to the Hellenistic period. At Saqqara recent excavations of catacombs in the region of the burial places of Isis and Imhotep have revealed several examples of mummified baboons, a creature sacred to Thoth and Imhotep, interred in wooden chests packed with gypsum plaster or cement (Emery 1970, 7).

At a later date in Egypt, mummification was certainly employed in a Christian context but apparently without the use of plaster. At the monastery of Epiphanius the bodies of the founding members of the community, buried beneath a later commemorative baldaquin, had been inhumed swathed in shrouds containing salt and juniper berry as embalming agents. (Cabrol and Leclerq 2, 2193). It also appears that embalming was employed by some early female monastic communities. (Palladius, ch. XXXIII).

In North Africa plaster burials seem to start in the 1st-3rd century BC and became recurrent features in Christian cemeteries of the 3rd-4th centuries AD. (Christoflé 1938, 131, 147). In the Christian cemeteries of Algeria and central Tunisia burials are consistently orientated with the head to the west, unaccompanied by grave goods, and placed in stone or tile cists or plain rectangular stone coffins, with flat or ridged tops. The bodies were often wrapped in a shroud, covered in plaster and enclosed in wooden or lead inner coffins (Gsell 1901, 396-412).

At Cherchel inscriptional evidence provides details of the organization of the cemetery. There, a senator, M Antonius Julius Severianus, had laid out an area of land outside the Roman city as a cemetery for his fellow Christians, with a *cella memoria* for himself and his family. Severianus had been a martyr, whose original monument had been destroyed; an inscription mentions its restoration (CIL, VIII, 9585). Another inscription from the same site refers to an *acubitorium,* a funerary monument containing several bodies and constructed for a priest (CIL, VIII, 9586).

These *areae* were separated and walled off from pagan cemeteries—plots of burial clubs, for instance—and contained the rich and poor lying side by side. Anniversary celebrations of martyrs and *agapes,* the funerary meals honouring the dead, were held there in the mausolea, which in the case of famous martyrs took the form of large basilicas with the altar over the martyr's tomb. Numerous such basilicas exist in North Africa, a reflection no doubt of the popularity of the veneration of the martyrs amongst the Donatist church.

At Tipasa the tomb of St Salsa, dating to the late 3rd or early 4th century, was soon the focus for an aisled chapel 15 m square with an apse on the east; this chapel was extended later to the west to double its former size, presumably in response to an increase in the congregation's size. Other smaller 4th century mausolea lay in the vicinity, containing the dead of important families not deserving commemoration by the community as a whole.

Surrounding these structures were numerous stone coffins, many of which contained bodies clothed in shrouds and laid in a bed of plaster, the coffin lids having been sealed with lead (Gsell 1901, 323-33; Christoflé 1938, 77). The family mausolea were normally small rectangular structures, with, in some cases, an apse at one end. These would hold the dead of one family over a period of two or three generations, but amongst the Donatists they might also act as places for the honouring of the martyrs, since relics were kept within them as protection for the humbler dead. Inside these structures a masonry platform, square or semi-circular in plan, acted as a table for the funeral banquet, while an altar might also be erected at one end over one of the more important graves. More elaborate types might be divided into nave and aisles, like the mausoleum of Bishop Alexander at Tipasa, the nave of which was decorated with mosaic floors including epitaphs of the dead, a common form of funerary art in North Africa. One of these mentions that not only Bishop Alexander but also the *iusti priores* (perhaps other Bishops of Tipasa) were interred here, their bodies lying in nine stone coffins forming a rostrum at the east end of the interior on which stood the altar. The majority of the eleven stone coffins were interred in the aisles, aligned with heads to the west. A semicircular masonry structure covered with mortar acted as table and seats for the funeral feasts (Gsell 1901, 333-7).

At Timgad further plaster burials are associated both with the Donatist cathedral and the large cemetery to the south-west of the town, where one such burial was the focus of a chapel, itself placed in the centre of the cemetery (Christoflé 1938, 369-70). At Carthage plaster burials seem not to have been recorded, but at the badly robbed site of the Basilica Majorium a group of burials placed beneath an altar set within an apse, included a child enclosed in a marble coffin, the body being surrounded by a black material which might, on analogy with other discoveries, be an embalming agent (Cabrol & Leclerq 2, 2233-61). These north African cemeteries demonstrate the widespread use of plaster burial, at least by some Christian communities, and also illustrate other elements in the funerary rite which recur with plaster burials at other cemeteries in Rome, the Rhineland, and Britain.

The main features of the Rome cemeteries have already been described, but referring to plaster burials in particular, two sites should be mentioned. In the Catacombs of Priscilla, one of the largest at Rome and founded in the 2nd century, all the bodies placed in *loculi* were enveloped in shrouds packed with plaster. In the cemetery of St Calixtus a family *hypogeum* contains two stone coffins in which lie embalmed bodies, and the uncorrupt state of St Cecilia's body when this was removed from a nearby chamber in the 9th century might suggest that her body had also been embalmed. However, preservation of the body may not have been the intention here; these could simply be measures to prevent the products of decomposition fouling the air in the confined underground space (Kirsch 1947, *passim*).

For the northern provinces the evidence is limited to the cities of north-east Gaul and the Rhineland, where the investigation of churches with early dedications has revealed a series of early Christian cemeteries.

At St Matthias, outside Trier, were buried SS Eucharius, Valerius, and Maternus, the bishops of Trier in the late 3rd century. None of their tombs, except perhaps that of Maternus, has been positively identified, but the excavations have revealed a large number of inhumations contained in stone coffins aligned east-west and rarely accompanied by gravegoods. The mausolea were simpler than those in north Africa and consisted of plain rectangular structures enclosing groups of stone coffins. One of these mausolea, under the west end of the present church, was aligned east-west, with the doorway at the east end, and measured c. 5 m by 4 m externally. The burials, in massive undecorated stone coffins, consisted of three adults and one child, two predating and two postdating the construction of the building. The burials all lay in earth-dug graves beneath the floor. Two of the coffins contained a few gravegoods of the 4th century, while that of the child contained a packing of plaster round the body (Cüppers 1965, 165-74). Individual burials were marked by marble inscriptions set horizontally over the grave, as in the Rome cemeteries (Cüppers 1965, 172).

At St Maximin's, beside the road north from Trier, another cemetery grew up round the burial place of Bishops Agritius and Maximinus. Under the present church has been identified the vault containing their remains and those of Nicetius, a later Bishop, while, outside, a large number of burials and two family mausolea have been excavated. The burials are of the usual type, enclosed in simple stone or wood coffins, occasionally accompanied by grave-goods of 4th century date, and and interred below the ancient ground level. Many of the coffins contained a plaster packing round the body, preserving the impression of the shroud, which in some cases was of gold-threaded cloth. Examination of the skeletal remains was claimed to show an unusually high percentage of people racially not native to western Europe, which may be of significance in view of the Mediterranean parallels already cited. Amongst the graves lay a small rectangular building c. 5 m by 6 m aligned east-west, and containing a single burial in a stone coffin. During the 4th century, on coin evidence, this building was replaced by a more elaborate structure, 6 m wide by 16 m long and divided into a *narthex* or vestibule at the east end, a main chamber, and an apse at the west end. Within the main chamber seventeen burials, including five in stone coffins, were inserted during the course of the 4th century.

Beside this mausoleum was a group of six burials, five in stone coffins, surrounded by five stone bases, the foundations for a funerary chapel of rather different character. Originally there would appear to have been seven or eight such bases, one at each corner and one in the middle of each side, supporting some structure c. 5 m square. The structure itself did not survive but the bases suggest a columnated building in the manner of the baldaquins erected in some Mediterranean cemeteries, such as that at the monastery of St Epiphanius in Egypt (see above).

Both at St Matthias and at St Maximin the buildings fell into neglect in the sub-Roman period, cist graves, possibly of Frankish settlers, being dug amongst their remains (Eiden 1958, 359-63).

Elsewhere in Trier, at St Medard's, what would appear to be another early Christian cemetery of a rather different and more mixed nature has come to light. Inhumations and one cremation were discovered laid out on a variety of alignments, some overlying earlier burials, and often accompanied by grave-goods in the form of pottery vessels. A lead-lined wooden coffin contained a body covered in plaster; as well as pottery and glass vessels and a box of jewellery. If this cemetery is indeed correctly identified as one of those used by the Christian community, it is a salutary reminder that the pagan customs died hard, and that in some cases Christian practices were not vigorously applied (Wightman 1970, 247).

Nearer the Rhine at Bonn and Xanten, further cemeteries have been identified, though differing in some respects from the Trier examples. Unlike Trier, Bonn was a city that shifted in the post-Roman period to focus on the actual site of the Christian cemetery. The focus of the cemetery consisted of the burials of two martyrs, Cassius and Florentinus, who were interred beside an earlier offering table (*mensa*) of north African type. The bodies were aligned with head to the south-west, as were those later interred in the vicinity in stone coffins. In the 4th century these burials were enclosed within rectangular mausolea to which three small antechambers had been added, one containing a burial overlain by a Christian inscription. Other inhumations around the mausoleum were contained in coffins or cists of stone, tile, or wood, the bodies aligned with head to the south-west, unaccompanied by grave-goods but in many cases surrounded by a plaster packing (Bader & Lehner 1932, 1-216).

At Xanten and Cologne similar cemeteries have been recorded but without apparently the employment of plaster burial. As at Bonn, orientation was often influenced by neighbouring roads, although there was a general tendency to place the head at the more westerly end of the grave (La Baume 1958, 42-47; Borger 1958, 380-90). Notwithstanding these local variations, the general character of these cemeteries is consistent and closely comparable to the customs already described from Rome and north Africa.

These German sites were all recognized from their location beneath churches dedicated to important figures in the early church. In Britain at least one such dedication exists at St Albans but has never been followed up by archaeological investigations, while others should exist at Caerleon, for instance, but have not yet been positively located (Radford 1971, 4). Cemeteries of the type associated with these sites on the continent have, however, been identified and have yielded both plaster burials and objects of an undoubtedly Christian nature. These sites have only been recognized as a result of casual discoveries, but in two cases they have been followed up by controlled excavations (Ramm 1971, 187-99).

Cemeteries in Britain

The cemetery at Poundbury lies on the outskirts of the present town of Dorchester (Dorset), the Roman Durnovaria and cantonal capital of the Durotriges. The total extent of the cemetery must be at least 1 ha and the number of burials approximately 4000, of which 1070 have been excavated. The origins of the cemetery lay in a small suburban settlement consisting of two simple courtyard houses and enclosures of 3rd century date. Associated with one house was a mixed cemetery of cremations and inhumations, the latter disposed on a variety of alignments and often accompanied by grave-goods of 3rd to early 4th century date. The earliest burials were frequently disturbed by later interments. At much the same time, in the courtyard of the other house, neat rows of unaccompanied inhumations, consistently oriented with head to the west, had been interred around a single special burial. The dead had been enclosed in wooden coffins, the special burial in a lead-lined coffin packed with plaster.

In the early 4th century this cemetery had encroached on the buildings and then expanded into a neighbouring enclosure. Here the dead were inhumed in similar fashion, arranged in serried ranks around a central cluster of nine lead-lined and one stone coffin. The latter and some of the ordinary wooden coffins contained a plaster packing.

In one corner of the enclosure two masonry mausolea overlay groups of plaster burials in lead and stone coffins. The mausolea were simple rectangular structures of mortared flint and measured 4 m by 6 m, the long side aligned east-west. One had been internally decorated with figured wall paintings and, from the occupation debris on the floor, had seen considerable use in the second quarter of the 4th century. The two lead coffins below the floor were of particular interest, since one bore on the underside of the lid the inscription I N DNE, *In Nomine [Tuo] Domine,* and in both remains of hair and possible embalming agents were present.

This cemetery had eventually spilled over into the neighbouring larger enclosure, which contained at least six similar mausolea besides numerous simple inhumations. Plaster burials were again encountered but with one exception were contained in wood or stone coffins. One mausoleum had been internally decorated with wall paintings depicting, at least in one part of the scheme, a group of seven male figures, two-thirds life-size, each holding a knobbed staff and clad in purple, white, or green robes or tunics. Other figures existed on the ceiling. The identity of the figures is uncertain; they may be members of the deceased family and holders of an office indicated by the knobbed staffs. The interior floor of this mausoleum bore the traces of intensive activity and yielded finds of the third quarter of the 4th century, including a coin re-used as a Christian amulet.

At the centre of this area was the inhumation of a man and two children, extended side by side and covered by a burnt wooden structure. No above-ground monument had survived but the central position and the dense cluster of graves at this point indicate that this burial was regarded as of some importance.

A further extension to the cemetery, containing at least two hamstone coffins, existed to the south-west, while over the whole site a second phase of burial has been recognized. This re-use consists of shallow inhumations, usually without coffins but also including occasional cist burials, the latter employing stonework robbed from the mausolea. This phase of the site is not closely dated but must fall in the late 4th century at the earliest. At a still later date a considerable settlement grew up in the centre of the cemetery.[2]

Near the west gate of the town another similar cemetery has been identified. Within an area of 0.7 ha a series of strictly oriented inhumations were recorded, including several enclosed in wooden coffins with iron angle-brackets, and two in lead-lined wooden coffins packed with gypsum. **One of the focal burials consisted of a young man** accompanied by remains of hair dressed in a pigtail, an interesting continuance of a Celtic hair-style amongst the **wealthier classes of late Roman provincial society. No** grave-goods were recovered from any of the graves, but from the close similarity to the early phase of the Poundbury cemetery a date in the first half of the 4th century can be suggested (Green, forthcoming).

These two cemeteries are both unlike the normal late Romano-British cemeteries round Dorchester, but yet are closely similar to the Christian cemeteries already described. Evidence for Christians in Roman Dorchester has, until now, been limited to a late hoard of silver spoons, but these cemeteries imply the presence of a large, well organized community from early in the 4th century and complements evidence for the influence of Christianity amongst the local villa owners. The previous lack of evidence need not be surprising: early churches are often difficult to recognize and inscriptions of any kind are rare in the area; indeed, the presence of Christian communities in cantonal capitals such as Dorchester would accord with the system on the continent and may yet prove to be the norm in this province.

The number of plaster burials at Dorchester is equalled only by the York cemeteries, where approximately 40 such burials have been recorded. The occurrence of gypsum burials in several of these cemeteries is of especial interest, since it is one place where a Christian community is known to have existed in the early 4th century, a bishop from this city being present, as a representative of *Britannia*

Secunda, at the Council of Arles in 314. The presence of the Constantinian family in York a few years previously, and the elevation of Constantine himself following his father's death in the same city, must have increased the prestige of the community in the years after the Peace of the Church. Unfortunately, the literary and epigraphic evidence gives no hint of the position of the churches or cemeteries.

York, however, can boast an extensive group of cemeteries containing plaster burials, the most important of these cemeteries covering an area of c. 6 ha north-west of colonia, on the site of the present railway station (RCHM 1962, 76-92). Accounts are obviously confused but from **the distribution of recorded burials the cemetery falls into** three parts: a 2nd-3rd century cremation cemetery in the south-west, an inhumation cemetery containing many stone and lead coffins, some with grave-goods, in the north-west, and the inhumation cemetery with plaster burials in the area outside the west gate and south-west corner of the colonia. In the latter area at least twenty plaster-packed lead or stone coffins were recorded, rarely accompanied by grave-goods. Mausolea were not recorded, although the grouping of the burials suggests such may have existed, and one female plaster burial lay in an underground vaulted chamber. In other cases burials may have been arranged in rows. The preferred orientation seems to have been with head to the west or north-west. Here, as at Bonn, a compromise has been made between the north-west/south-east alignment of the road grid and a strict east-west orientation, the head being placed at the more westerly end of the grave.

Burials containing grave-goods are frequently reported but would anyway tend to excite interest and therefore to be recorded at the expense of the mass of simple inhumations. Of the provenanced pottery, much belongs to the cremation **cemetery and is of 2nd-3rd century date. Where grave-** goods are recorded in the plaster burial cemetery they mostly take the form of jewellery accompanying rich female burials, a situation paralleled at Poundbury. Grave markers were observed, especially in the area of the plaster burial cemetery outside the west gate, the marker in one case including a broken pagan altar. This and the re-use of coffins here and at the Castle Yard has been taken as indicative of a 'social revolution' connected with reorganization of the army and the disorders of the late 3rd century. Another possibility must also be considered, that the desecration of these pagan burials was at the hands of the Christian community, the re-use of the altar and the coffins being symbolic of paganism's defeat. One burial was recorded as being furnished with a bone plaque inscribed DOMINE VICTOR VINCAS FELIX, an invocation, surely, with Christian overtones, and recalling the well known Christian inscription from another cemetery in Bootham Terrace, north-west of the fortress (RCHM 1962, 135, no. 149, pl. 65). In that case a woman in a stone coffin, without plaster packing, was accompanied by a bone plaque, inscribed SOROR AVE VIVAS IN DEO and other jewellery (RCHM 1962, 73, fig. 58).

Other sites in York have produced plaster burials in small numbers, principally the Castle Yard, south-east of the fortress, and the Mount, south of the colonia. Both sites are only imperfectly known and have produced a variety of burials; the plaster burials were in several instances in re-used inscribed or decorated coffins and, where recorded, aligned with head to the north-west (RCHM 1962, 95-100; Ramm 1971, 190-1). One gypsum burial occurred at Trentholme Drive in an irregularly

planned cemetery of 350 inhumations and cremations accompanied by grave-goods (Wenham 1968, 40-2).

In comparison with York, London has surprisingly few examples, concentrated mainly in a cemetery in Old Ford on the Colchester road east of the city. The twelve plaster-packed lead or stone coffins from the site were generally unaccompanied by grave-goods but were variously aligned and associated with other accompanied cremations and inhumations (RCHM 1928, 164; Owen et al. 1973, 135-45). The inscribed coffin from Westminster Abbey originally contained a plaster burial, before its re-use in the medieval period, but whether this had been derived from an earlier cemetery at Westminster or elsewhere is unknown (Stanley 1870, 103-28).

In the south-east of the province several isolated plaster burials have been recorded, of which two are worthy of mention. Overlooking the villa at Lullingstone (Kent) a mausoleum in the form of a Romano-Celtic temple was erected over two burials dating to the late 3rd or early 4th century. One burial had been removed in the late 4th century but the remaining example, a lead coffin decorated with scallop shell and cable ornament, contained the remains of a man packed in plaster. The north-south alignment, the presence of grave-goods, and the form of the monument all appear non-Christian, but the later establishment in the nearby villa of a chapel decorated with funerary wall-paintings, the removal of one body from the mausoleum, and the re-use of the structure as a church in the Saxon period could suggest that the dead were of some Christian significance (Richmond 1959, 132-3; Radford 1971, 6; personal information from Lt-Col G W Meates).

A plaster burial of a woman in the inhumation cemetery at Dartford had preserved not only the hair gathered on the crown of the head and fastened by a bandeau of pearls, but also remnants of an aromatic substance, possibly an embalming agent. A coin associated with this burial dated to the second quarter of the 4th century (VCH Kent, **3**, 89).

Finally, the site at Icklingham in Suffolk deserves to be considered. Numerous discoveries over the last two centuries have revealed the presence of an unwalled town of approximately 15 ha, surrounded by cemeteries, including one in the south-east which has produced numerous burials of Christian type, mausolea and plaster burials, and at least one lead tank decorated with the Christian monogram (VCH **1**, 309; *Antiq. Journ.* 22 (1942), p. 219; *Britannia* **3**, (1972), 330). The most important of the 19th century discoveries was a group of four burials comprising two in stone coffins, one in a lead-lined wooden coffin and a further uncoffined burial. The burials were crammed into an area c. 2.5 m by 3.5 m surrounded by traces of an enclosing building, largely robbed away. Of the stone coffins, one was sealed with pink concrete and contained remains of an adult male, while the other lacked the sealing but contained the remains of an adult male packed in plaster. The lead coffin lay alongside and enclosed the body of a woman. All three burials were extended with head to the west and were not accompanied by grave-goods. The fourth burial lay to the east, aligned at right-angles as if crammed into the remaining space at the east end of a now destroyed mausoleum. In this instance the body had been placed, unaccompanied by grave-goods, in a simple dug grave covered by a tile pavement (Prigg 1901, 65-71).

Of the three lead tanks, the most recently discovered came to light within a hundred yards of the possible mausoleum described above and was itself surrounded by structural remains. Excavations in 1974, prompted by these discoveries, showed that the building had been too badly robbed for the plan to be recovered, apart from a small tile- and plaster-lined apse but did reveal an inhumation cemetery and two other buildings in the immediate vicinity. The buildings were rectangular in plan, c. 5 m x 8 m, constructed of flints and mortar and aligned along the same east-west axis. No burials were contained within them but in the surrounding area numerous inhumations were recorded, aligned approximately east-west and unaccompanied by grave-goods other than occasional ironwork from biers or coffins.[3]

Other urban centres in Britain have produced little or no evidence of plaster burial cemeteries, although at Gloucester the Kingsholm cemetery has produced lead and stone coffins and many others with a 'lime packing' (Fosbrooke 1819). The strange diversity of sites represented here is, however, simply a reflection of recent excavation; until their investigation the Dorchester and Icklingham cemeteries consisted of only isolated, badly recorded plaster burials, while the York cemetery is only known because of its wholesale destruction. Many plaster burials may have escaped notice in the past, for over a period of 1500 years in the north European climate and soil conditions both lime and gypsum plaster can be dissolved, where not protected by a stone or lead container. It is becoming clear that at Poundbury many wooden coffined burials yield minute traces of plaster and that, at this site and others, many if not most of the burials had originally been accorded this treatment.

Conclusion

In this cursory survey of the evidence from only part of the Western Empire similarities have been pointed out between the physical remains of some known Christian cemeteries. These features also recur in other cemeteries for which documentary or topographical evidence is lacking but which nevertheless should be considered as the burial places for Christian communities not otherwise recognized. Not all plaster burials occur in Christian contexts and they are not the sole feature distinguishing these cemeteries from others, but they are distinctive features which may pinpoint possible sites. Where they both occur in numbers and coincide with other features of Christian burial practice the foregoing examples would suggest such sites are Christian. Plaster burial is an exotic custom transmitted across the Empire by the spread of an exotic religion and is a rite of significance only to the followers of that faith.

Plaster burials should, though, be considered in the context of the systematic study of burial types in a cemetery, their relative frequency, the layout and development of the graveyard, the character of any monuments, and the cemeteries' relationship to the surrounding pattern of rural and/or suburban settlement. Individual burials, richly furnished or exceptional in other respects, are less important than the norm, the general rite of burial characterizing the community and its attitude to the dead. Such an approach will only yield results in the future as more cemeteries, both Christian and pagan, are studied. Where large samples of well preserved skeletal remains can be recovered such sites will illustrate, besides the religious beliefs, the standard of health, the living conditions, and the social structure of the population. Already surprising results are being obtained on lead ingestion in Romano-British populations (Waldron, Mackie, and Townshend

1976, 221-7). Much of this is information that cannot be retrieved from other sources and will complement the archaeological record obtained from settlement sites.

In the western provinces as a whole and Britain in particular there has been little success in identifying the physical remains of Christianity, the churches and baptisteries which might complement the meagre literary sources and allow the impact of the new religion to be assessed. This may not be pure chance but a reflection of the limited church building carried out before the 5th century anywhere in the Roman world, with the notable exception of the structures erected under Imperial patronage (Duval, 1975, passim). Cemeteries may, then, be the foci for other activities than simply the burial and commemoration of the dead, as is suggested by the finds at Icklingham. Such sites may, indeed, be the only physical evidence for the existence of some communities; they will, at the very least, provide a fuller understanding of the development and organization of the Church in the Western Empire.

Notes

1   In the study of these burials I must gratefully acknowledge the great assistance and advice I have received from Ray Farrar, Herman Ramm, and Dr John Peter Wild. In particular, I owe to Ray Farrar the suggestion that the Poundbury cemetery was Christian and much encouragement in the initial stages of the work. In this paper the term 'gypsum burial' or 'lime burial' will be limited to those occasions where there is direct evidence for the particular material used. Where doubt exists or where the rite is referred to only in general terms the term 'plaster burial' will be used.
2   Casual discoveries on the site and the results of excavations until 1967 are summarized in the Royal Commission on Historical Monuments (1970) Vol. II, *South East Dorset*, part 3, 583-5, monument 225. Interim reports have been published annually in the *Proceedings of the Dorset Natural History and Archaeological Society* for the years 1966-75. For details of the wall paintings in mausoleum R9, see 'The Funerary Wall Paintings and Cemetery at Poundbury, Dorchester, Dorset', Unpublished BA thesis, Institute of Archaeology, University of London, May 1971.
3   I am indebted to Stanley West, Director of the Suffolk Archaeological Unit, for information on this site prior to publication.

Bibliography

Bader, W, and Lehner, H (1932) 'Baugeschichtliche Untersuchungen am Bonner Münster' *Bonner Jahrb* **136/7**, 1-216
Borger, H (1958) 'Die Ausgrabungen im Bereich des Xantener Domes' in *Neue Ausgrabungen in Deutschland* (Berlin: Gebr. Mann)
Cabrol, F, and Leclerq, H (1907-53) *Dictionnaire d'Archéologie Chrétienne et de Liturgie* (Paris, Letonzey et Ané)
Christoflé (ed) (1938) *Rapport sur les Travaux de Fouilles et Consolidations Effectuées en 1933-6 par le Service des Monuments Historiques de l'Algérie*
Clarke, G N (1972) 'Lankhills School' *Antiq. J.* **52**, 94-8
Cüppers, H (1965) 'Das Gräberfeld von St Matthias' in Reusch, W (ed), *Frühchristliche Zeugnisse*
Duval, N (1975) 'Edifices de culte des origines à l'époque constantinienne', *Atti IX Congresso Internazionale di Archeologia Cristiana* (Rome)
Eiden, H (1958) 'Ausgrabungen im spätantiken Trier' in *Neue Ausgrabungen in Deutschland* (Berlin: Gebr. Mann)
Emery, W B (1970) 'Preliminary report on excavations at N. Saqqara, 1969-70' *J. Egyptian Archaeol.* **56**, 5-11
Espérandieu, E (1938) *Recueil General des Bas-Releifs, Statues et Bustes de la Gaule Romaine*, **11**, (Paris)
Fosbrooke, T D (1819) *History of the City of Gloucester*
Gose, E (1958) *Katalog der Frühchristliche Inschriften aus Trier*
Green, C J S (forthcoming) 'The Crown Buildings Cemetery, Dorchester, Dorset' in Putnam, W G (ed), *Dorchester Excavations*, **1**
Gsell, A (1901) *Monuments Antiques de l'Algérie*, **2**
Jones, A H M (1962) *Constantine and the Conversion of Europe* (London)
Kirsch, G P (1947) *Catacombs of Rome*

La Baume, P (1958) *Cologne, Colonia Agrippinensis*

Lethbridge, T C (1936) 'Further excavations in the Early Iron Age and Romano-British cemetery at Guilden Morden' *Proc. Cambridge Antiq. Soc.* **36,** 109-20

Nock, A D (1932) 'Cremation and burial in the Roman Empire' *Harvard Theol. Rev.* **25**

Owen, W J, Schwab, I, and Sheldon, H (1973) 'Roman burials from Old Ford' *Trans. London Middlesex Archaeol. Soc.* **24,** 135-45

Prigg, H (1901) *Icklingham Papers*

Radford, C A R (1971) 'Christian origins in Britain' *Medieval Archaeol.* **15,** 1-12

Ramm, H G (1971) 'The end of Roman York' in Butler, R M (ed), *Soldier and Civilian in Roman Yorkshire*

Richmond, I A (1950) Archaeology and the Afterlife in pagan and Christian Imagery

Richmond, I A (1959) Roman Britain in 1958 in J. Roman Stud., 49

RCHM (1928) Royal Commission on Historical Monuments (England) *An Inventory of Historical Monuments in London 4—Roman London* (London: HMSO)

RCHM (1962) Royal Commission on Historical Monuments (England). An Inventory of Historical Monuments in the City of York. 1—Eburacum, Roman York (London: HMSO)

Stanley, A R (1870) 'Observations on the Roman sarcophagus lately discovered at Westminster' *Archaeol. J.* **27,** 103-9

Testini, P (1966) *Le Catacombe e gli Antiche Cimiteri Cristiani in Roma*

Toynbee, J M C (1968) 'Pagan motifs and practices in Christian art and ritual in Roman Britain' in Barley, M W, and Hanson, R P C (eds) *Christianity in Britain, 300-700,* 177-92 (Leicester: University Press)

Toynbee, J M C (1971) *Death and Burial in the Roman World* (London: Thames and Hudson)

Viner, D J (1973) 'The cemeteries. in McWhirr, A D, 'Cirencester, 9th Interim Report, 1969-73' *Antiq. J.* **43,** 191-218

Waldron, H A, Mackie, A, and Townshend, A (1976) 'The lead content of some Romano-British bones' *Archaeometry* **18**

Wenham, L P (1968) *The Romano-British Cemetery at Trentholme Drive, York* (London: HMSO)

Wightman, E (1970) *Roman Trier and the Treveri* (London: Hart-Davis)

Zwisa (ed) (   ) *Corpus Scriptorum Ecclesiasticorum Latinorum* **26,** St Optatus

Late Roman cemeteries and beyond

Philip Rahtz

Introduction

This paper is an exploratory attempt to define and classify a class of inhumation cemetery in Roman and later Britain. These are characterized by a predominantly west-east orientation and by an absence or paucity of grave goods, and yet not in obviously Christian contexts. Most seem to be late or immediately post-Roman, but there is some evidence that the class begins in earlier Roman or even in prehistoric times—or at any rate that the earliest phases of some cemeteries may extend back into these centuries. Whether Roman or later, there are often Roman features, including some grave-associated objects and residual material.

The class is neither obviously Roman nor clearly related to the English settlement; there is no direct evidence that any are Christian or pagan, though the general characteristics are conventionally regarded as more appropriate to the former. Thus, by definition, Roman Christian cemeteries like Poundbury would be excluded, though its secondary post-Roman graves would be included; so, too, would the class exclude cemeteries like Whitby or Church Island, in an English or western British monastic context, and those like Winnall II (Meaney and Hawkes 1970) or Leighton Buzzard (Hyslop 1963), which are believed to represent the Christianizing phase of English mortuary practice. Late Roman pagan cemeteries with grave-goods such as Winchester (Lankhills) would not be in this class, nor would any 'pagan' Saxon cemetery, even though these cemeteries share certain characteristics with those under review.

This leaves a considerable number of cemeteries; the group considered in this paper are only the most obvious, a sample culled mainly from the six numbers of *Britannia*, and from *Medieval Archaeology*; further research would greatly increase their number. Several of those in Somerset have come to light in the course of Ian Burrow's work on Somerset hilltops; I am grateful to him for supplying the details of these in this paper.

The class was originally defined in a narrower sense by Phillips (OS Dark Age Map 1966) as 'sub-Roman', a classification followed by Rahtz (1968). These preliminary attempts at definition were restricted to western Britain, particularly to Somerset, which still provides some of the most characteristic examples in the present paper. They were described as being 'of the immediately post-Roman period in areas fully Romanised in the fourth century, but where there is a long gap between the breakdown of central Roman authority and the establishment of Saxon settlement' (Rahtz 1968). Such cemeteries in Somerset seemed to fit into a *lacuna* which in that area is of three centuries' duration. The wider implications of the class in relation to other aspects of Somerset settlement were further discussed in 1972 (Rahtz and Fowler 1972). The variety of cemetery. even in this small group made their inclusion in a single class called vaguely 'sub-Roman' patently simplistic. The concept and area were both too narrow, and the 1974 seminar offered an opportunity and a stimulus to expand the discussion, though not with any useful results.

Four types (A-D) are here proposed; limitations in our understanding severely undermine their credibility as valid historical concepts.

There is obviously much overlap, both culturally and chronologically, between the types and uncertainty about the type to which a particular cemetery should be assigned, and between the types as a class and those that have been excluded. The attempt at classification may, however, stimulate more systematic work on this topic, and at least suggest that there are unresolved problems. These may be summarized as follows:

1   To what extent are such cemeteries part of an indigenous cultural tradition which begins in prehistoric times, and extends through the Roman

period and beyond; or do they develop as a response to external (i.e. continental) stimuli; or are they mainly a *de novo* development during the Roman period or later?

2   To what extent are they Christian in origin or development, or a continuance of a pagan tradition of west-east findless graves?

3   Can they always be distinguished from monastic or other definitely Christian cemeteries of later date, of **e.g. the 7th-8th centuries and later? (Compare the difficulty in separating monastic from secular settlements) (Rahtz 1973).**

4   In what ways may such cemeteries reflect the socio-economic character of their associated settlements?

5   What does the evidence of their size and distribution contribute to demographic studies?

No 'answers' are suggested in this paper, but the statement of problems may suggest the directions in which further research might be pursued. (Site names in italics are those listed in Table I.)

West-east orientation and sparsity of grave-goods

West-east orientated cemeteries with few or no grave-goods are not exclusively of post-Roman date, nor are they necessarily Christian. The question of orientation is one which has not been seriously explored in this country; as in many topics, the last word on this was said by Baldwin Brown (1915, 162 etc.) His conclusion, which there is still no reason to challenge, is that north-south or random orientation is most likely to be pagan, and that west-east orientation, while characteristic of many[1] Christian cemeteries, owes nothing to primary Christian belief, but was adopted and rationalized[2] from a common pagan practice. This would seem to be confirmed in respect of this class of cemetery by any case where the cemetery can be shown to be pre-Christian in date, as seems to be the case at *Cannington*. It seems probable that an increasing tendency to west-east orientation in an indigenous pagan context was accelerated and regularized by its adoption by Christians. Yet west-east orientation is still commonly accepted as evidence of Christianity (e.g. by Wilson 1968) or implicitly **in the discussions on Christianizing phases of Saxon** cemeteries (e.g. Hyslop 1963 or Meaney and Hawkes 1970).

Sparsity of grave-goods can similarly be 'explained' by reference to Christian belief, but is also common in Roman and earlier cemeteries. Nor is the presence of grave-goods inconsistent with Christianity. Especially in Merovingian Christian graves, or in later Christian Moravian ones, grave-goods are as rich as those in pagan graves. Salin (1952, 236) discussed the former, and the extent to which grave-goods were related to status as homage or insignia, or as accessories to clothing rather **than as provision for an after-life.**[3] **The dangers inherent in** too facile an interpretation of the function of grave-goods have recently been stressed by Ucko (1969). The best example of a 'well-furnished' Christian in this country is St Cuthbert, who was buried (or shortly afterwards reburied) in a decorated coffin, in which were not only costly vestments (Bede) but objects which may all have been insignia (pectoral cross, portable altar, comb, and scissors with gold, silver, and garnets), rather than personal possessions. It is interesting that Bede described his burial and, eleven years later, his exhumation and

reburial, as a contemporary observer; he mentions the old and new coffins and vestments, but not any of the contemporary objects later found in the coffin. Notable objects are also common in the graves of medieval ecclesiastics such as those recently found in York Minster (Ramm 1971).

The absence of grave-goods in either Christian or pagan contexts can be explained by the poverty of the associated settlement, by its unwillingness to relinquish useful objects, or by a religious belief or custom which deplored the practice—a situation which generally, though not exclusively, prevails in England today. Such a tendency is evident in Europe, especially in the late Roman period, even in 'wealthy' graves (e.g. Bathstone coffin burials), and may similarly have been adopted and regularized by Christianity.

West-east findless graves may thus be present in Roman contexts. Where they are later than the Edict of Toleration (313) they may, of course, be Christian; it is perhaps surprising that, of all late Roman cemeteries, only Poundbury has yielded unequivocal Christian evidence. For the others listed here, the religious connotations are 'unproven', even though sometimes claimed (*Ancaster*).

Summary of types, with suggested examples

A   Sub-Roman: secular villa, town or other settlement contexts

Ancaster
Banwell
Beacon Hill
Bletsoe
Bradley Hill (W-E group)
Bray
Caerwent
Camerton
Cirencester
Doulting
Dorchester (Oxon.)
Eccles
Eccleston
Knockea
Llantwit Major
Portishead
Poundbury (latest phase)
Stretton-on-the-Fosse
Welton Wold
Winchester (Victoria Road)
Wint Hill

B   Sub-Roman religious sites

Blaise Castle
Brean Down
Cannington
Frilford
Henley Wood
Icklingham
Lamyatt Beacon
Weycock Hill

C   Associated with hill-top settlements

? Blaise Castle
Cannington
Daw's Castle
Henley Wood
King's Weston Down
Maiden Castle

Poundbury (latest phase)
Weston-super-Mare (Worlebury)
(Worlebury)

D   Early Christian sites

Hartlepool
? Llandegai
Lundy
Monkwearmouth
Jarrow
(see also Thomas 1971)

Type A—Sub-Roman secular

This group comprises cemeteries which appear to be secondary to Roman contexts: most in fact appear to be late or post-Roman. Where a 'late Roman' date is claimed (i.e. in the 4th or early 5th century), it is usually on the fallacious basis of dating by late Roman pottery or coins, which can only usually give a *terminus post quem* (cf. Rahtz and Fowler 1972, 191); the point was underlined by the finding at Cadbury-Congresbury in 1973 of a 'freshly broken' Roman pot in association with a sherd of north African pot dated independently to *c.* 525.

In most cases, a 5th century or later Roman date is either claimed (*Bray, Caerwent, Dorchester, Eccles, Poundbury, Welton Wold*) or seems possible or even likely. Their inclusion in type A is usually on the basis of a direct association with a Roman site, or because of the presence of Roman finds, whether residual or not. In some cases (*Ancaster, Bray, Cirencester, Dorchester, Winchester (Victoria Road)*), this Roman association can hardly be challenged. In other cases (*Bradley Hill* west-east group, *Eccles, Stretton-on-the-Fosse*) such an association seems probable, but there are others (*Beacon Hill, Camerton, Llantwit Major, Welton Wold*) where it is more dubious. Where a Roman background is accepted, the cemetery may well be seen as that of the community continuing into post-Roman decades or centuries; where it is not, the occurrence of a cemetery on or near a Roman site, or with Roman material in the graves, may be indirect or even coincidental. The possibility of many of type A being of substantially post-Roman date is perhaps currently obscured by their record being embedded in the annals of Roman archaeology. Most of my examples were in *Britannia*, but very few in *Medieval Archaeology!*

Most of type A are near Roman villas or towns, where they are more likely to be found in excavation. Others, in poorer rural contexts (e.g. *Beacon Hill, Portishead*) will only be found where areas are stripped for other reasons.

A distinction should be made in type A between those cemeteries which seem to be *de novo* (e.g. *Bletsoe, Dorchester, Eccles, Portishead*) and those which comprise later phases of an existing cemetery, whether on the same site (e.g. *Ancaster, Poundbury, Stretton-on-the-Fosse*) or close by (e.g. *Bradley Hill* west-east group). The latter are presumably more likely to be indicative of continuity of settlement/burial than the former.

Type A cemeteries are mainly of west-east graves, with few finds. It excludes some with few finds except boot-nails, and others with severed heads, usually between legs or feet (e.g. *Beckford, Stretton-on-the-Fosse* earlier cemetery). These two facets may prove to be significant in this discussion; either or both may be sub- or post-Roman. In one case (*Stretton-on-the-Fosse*) the type A cemetery is secondary to a 'boot-cemetery'. Some of type A have features which are more common in Roman contexts.

Such are coffin-nails (*Ancaster, Dorchester*), or wood or stone coffins or slabs (*Ancaster, Bletsoe*). These are perhaps earlier than those in which no such features are present; at *Bradley Hill*, the type A cemetery is apparently secondary to another with such features apparently dated to the late Roman period.

Type A is thus a varied group, and the adjective 'sub-Roman' only the loosest of blanket labels.

Type B—Sub-Roman religious

These are similar to type A, except insofar as they are on sites with religious buildings or structures; further excavation of type A sites might, of course, reveal such structures. Where a cemetery is associated with a temple or shrine, it need not, of course, be directly linked with a nearby community, but perhaps be drawn from several local groups, or perhaps from even further afield. Burial on sacred sites is not a universal phenomenon, and where it does take place it may be indicative of a particular cult or custom. Type B excludes cemeteries on religious sites which are clearly Roman; such seems to be the case with at least the earlier phases of *Cannington*, though this cemetery must be considered as a whole.

Blaise Castle may be late Roman and probably secondary to a temple but the others appear to be at least partly post-Roman. *Henley Wood* is secondary to a temple, and is possibly that of the nearby 6th century settlement of Cadbury—Congresbury (Rahtz and Fowler 1972, 192ff). *Brean Down* has one radiocarbon date centring in the 6th century, but its association with the nearby temple is speculative, though there was certainly some activity on the site of the latter in the 5th century. At *Frilford* there is also an Anglo-Saxon cemetery close by. At *Lamyatt Beacon*, west-east graves were secondary to a temple, and on a different alignment.

Direct association in time and place with a pagan religious site must, of course, imply that the cemetery is pagan, but either the site or the cemetery may later become Christian; such may be the case at both *Cannington* and *Henley Wood*, but the possibility must be considered that Roman religious sites may have continued as pagan sacred sites well into the 5th and 6th centuries or even later.

Icklingham is associated with a religious site, but not exclusively a pagan one like those above; there are specifically Christian finds from the site, including the well known lead tank; the cemetery may, however, be neither Christian nor of the late Roman date claimed for the complex as a whole.

Type C—Associated with hilltop settlements

The examples in this type are all in Somerset or Dorset, and there may be many others of this class. In no case can association with the settlement be proved, but if it is accepted, then these cemeteries are of settlements that are certainly not Roman in any conventional sense. Hilltop settlements, mostly in hillforts, are usually considered, in England at least, to be *de novo* establishments in a society reverting to Iron Age styles of living in the 5th or later centuries (Fowler 1971). There is some evidence, however, that hilltop settlement as a phenomenon is not exclusively post-Roman, even in England; the evidence for the *Cannington* cemetery may be cited in support of this, if the cemetery *is* that of the hilltop settlement. A possibility is emerging that use of hillforts or other hills may not be as secular as the proposed militaristic model of (e.g.) South Cadbury might presuppose. A religious interpretation might indeed be more appropriate to type C cemeteries (especially *Blaise Castle, Henley Wood,* and *Cannington*), which would incline them towards type B; this does not, of course, preclude their being related to hilltop settlements. In the case of *Cannington* such a double equation, with religious site and hillfort, has been made, and the suggested order of size of the cemetery (2000-5000 graves), has been used as direct demographic evidence of the order of size of the settlement in or around Cannington hillfort. If such a direct equation could be proved between the apparently complete cemetery at *Henley Wood* and that of Cadbury-Congresbury, the population of the latter was small indeed!

Type D—Early Christian sites

These are on Christian sites but not necessarily part of them. Their occurrence on Christian sites does, however, suggest that they may be Christian. The earliest cemeteries at *Monkwearmouth* and *Jarrow* are, for instance, apparently earlier than the earliest monastic structures which are at present definable; they are apparently lay cemeteries and possibly pre-Saxon. If they are Christian, there may, of course, be a direct association between them and the location of the monastery; the same may be true of *Lundy* and other sites described by Thomas (1971, ch. 3). The latter include those defined by Thomas as 'undeveloped', Christian cemeteries that did not continue in use long enough for specifically Christian structures, such as chapels, to become their nuclei. There is no direct evidence that these cemeteries were Christian, although Thomas considers them to be 'the primary field-monuments of insular Christianity' (1971, 50).

Other cemeteries in the whole class discussed in this paper may have features which could, but need not, be interpreted as Christian. Thus at *Cannington,* the girl's grave (409) may be a secondary Christian nucleus (below, 58), while *Henley Wood* may be linked with the tenuous evidence for pagan/Christian transition at Cadbury-Congresbury.

Conclusion: Methodology

The confusion evident in the foregoing pages reflect the difficulties in interpreting a class of cemeteries that have no secure dating or cultural affiliation. The main problem is that of *dating.* Dates for a few graves are given by grave-goods, but more usually there is only a *terminus post quem* based on residual material or stratigraphical relationships. The only hope of assigning cemeteries even to a particular century, if they have a short life, or of assessing their range, seems to lie in radiocarbon dating. Dates obtained so far on cemeteries of this class are only of a single skeleton (*Dorchester, Brean Down*) or of a few (*Cannington*) and in neither case is this enough. At Westerhus, in a later period, about 3% were assayed (12 of 364) and this was sufficient, not only to confirm the general 'historical' dating of the cemetery (in the 12th-13th centuries), but also to enable important and unexpected conclusions to be made about the multi-nuclear development of the cemetery rather than the linear sequence that had been postulated (Gejvall 1960 and 1968). The five *Cannington* determinations are the main evidence on which the cemetery is dated, but they posed as many problems as they solved and their validity, especially that of the earlier dates (see below, 58) would be

strengthened by many more determinations. More experimental work is needed to check the validity of basic method (the *Cannington* dates were recently moved over a century earlier as a result of re-assessment of method by the Birmingham radiocarbon laboratory), such as the relationship between radiocarbon intake and date of death, apart from the subtleties of calibration. A large research programme is currently being done by the Winchester Research Unit, based on a comparison of ^{14}C in bone content and that of associated charcoal, in 'charcoal burials' of the later Saxon period; this may help in the assessment of all cemetery determinations.

Another major limitation in the understanding of these cemeteries is the small scale of the excavation. Few of the cemeteries described here are complete (*Bradley Hill,* ? *Henley Wood*), though the extent of others may be gauged (*Dorchester, Cannington, Poundbury*). Nor do we always know the character or even location of the associated settlement; larger area excavations are needed.

Nor is the quality of excavation good enough; the presence of a human biologist on the excavation staff (e.g. *Poundbury*) is still a rarity; recording is often not good enough to permit exhaustive analysis of data such as attitude, orientation, superimposition, and exact find-spots (cf. Struever 1971).

Finally, stress should be laid on the historical importance of the excavation of cemeteries of this class. There has been a certain reluctance to excavate cemeteries which do not produce finds, and a reluctance on the part of those financing excavation to sponsor them. What was left of *Cannington* by 1962 would not have been excavated because of its intrinsic interest as a cemetery (which was stressed at the time, though without full realization of its ultimate implications), but because Don Brothwell wished to have a good sample of skeletons of the area and period and threw in his moral support. The excavation of part of the *Dorchester* cemetery was done in haste, without adequate resources, and it is doubtful whether the Oxford archaeologists would have received enough support to excavate the 700 or so graves which probably existed, even if their existence and the extent of the threat had been recognized.

Post-Roman cemeteries are an essential part of settlement studies of the 5th to 7th centuries; the main value of the monograph on *Cannington* will be to show not just the interest attaching to that particular cemetery, but the *kind* of evidence that such a cemetery *could* produce if it were totally and scientifically excavated. What this amounted to in the case of *Cannington* will finally be summarized, though no adequate summary can be made of the difficult evidence that the site produced, which has taken nearly ten years to bring to any form, and that by no means a satisfactory one.

The Cannington cemetery

The excavation of 1962-63 recovered evidence of 523 individuals in advance of quarrying; most of the cemetery had already gone, but estimates of area and density based on earlier observations suggest an original size of 2000-5000. Two major limitations prevent any satisfactory interpretation: one is the incompleteness of the part excavated (though it may include the nuclei); the other is the excessive 'background noise' of settlement material, which includes much prehistoric, Roman, and a little post-Roman material, some of which must be contemporary

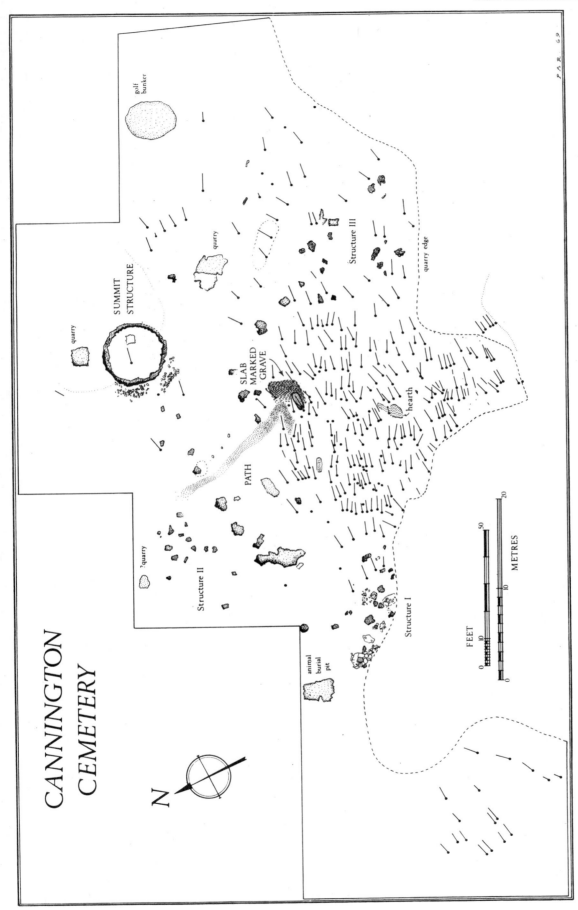

CANNINGTON
CEMETERY

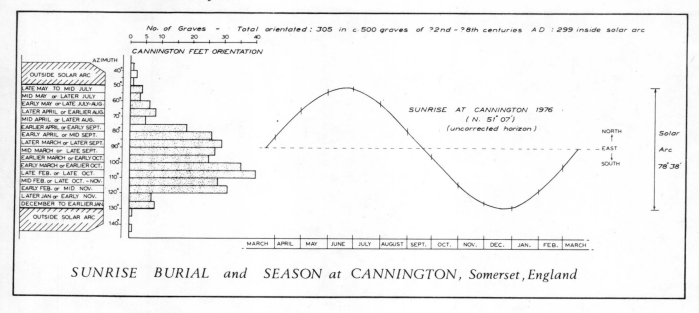

2   *Sunrise, burial, and season at Cannington (Somerset)*

with at least one phase of the cemetery. It includes definite non-grave material, such as industrial waste. It was impossible to decide what of this material was grave-goods, and what was residual, though the Roman and later finds do give *termini post quem* for individual graves. The only objects likely to be grave-goods are about a dozen knives, a few shroud-pins of copper alloy or bone, and two infant grave-groups. One of these comprised a perforated coin of Allectus, a western British ?post-Roman silver bracelet, and an amber bead. Close by, the other consisted of a glass bead with 'string' inserts of Irish type, and a tri-lobed brooch dated to the 7th or 8th century; the dating of this grave may carry the other with it. Analysis of the distribution of grave-goods was not positive, though several of the knives and the two infants were in an area of more isolated graves towards the south-east side of the cemetery. Radiocarbon dates (uncorrected)[4] centre on ad 153, 228, 468, 518, and 620 (revised half-lives would make these dates rather earlier. The cemetery then would seem to extend from early or mid-Roman times to the 7th or 8th century.

The cemetery (Fig. 1) has some positive edges, beyond which were 'taboo' areas where there are only isolated graves. There are numerous post-holes and other features; some of these may be pre-cemetery, but some seem to represent structures which are part of the cemetery complex, notably 'across' what seems to be the approach to the cemetery. There are two important nuclei in the area dug; on the summit of the hill, away from the densest areas of the cemetery, is a circular trench cut in the rock with a ?polygonal setting of imported stones around it. This is interpreted as a Roman or sub-Roman shrine or temple building, though other interpretations, especially that of a mausoleum, are equally possible. Near the centre was a grave (radiocarbon dates of ad 468 and 518) which might be earlier, contemporary, or later stratigraphically. The other nucleus is close to the edge of the grave area; the grave (no. 409) of a young girl (radiocarbon date of ad 620) was covered by a mound, in the surface of which the position of the grave was marked by a setting of imported stone. Subsequently the mound was much visited, and a clearly defined path led from it towards the north.

Several later graves had cut into the mound; one, a crouched burial, had even removed stones from the setting to make a rough cist. The girl's grave was orientated exactly due west-east.

Twenty-eight graves appeared to have a lining, rather like a cist-grave, some with imported stone. Single isolated graves tended to be deeper than those in dense areas; most depths were 15-50 cm into the bedrock. Three skeletons were crouched and 294 extended. Forty-four had arms flexed across the waist, fourteen extended fully by the sides, and fourteen flexed to the neck; the latter position was also recorded by earlier observers, and might be a specifically Christian trait.

Analysis of orientation of 305 graves (Fig. 2) showed a divergence of 55° either side of 270°, but the average was 276°; 299 of these fell within the solar arc (230-310°) of this latitude, which suggests that observation of sunrise was a major factor in determining orientation, and 258 fell within the narrower arc of 255-300°. While season of death may be at least one factor, there may have been others. The only structure which could have guided orientation was the slab-marked mound.

One orientation model suggested that the cemetery might be of two broad groupings, a small one with heads predominantly south of west, and the other around the average north of west. Another was erected on a three-group concept, a central one close to the 'desirably orientated' girl's grave, and a group to either side of this. Such evidence of superimposition of graves as there was was not positive, but hinted at the possibility that south-turning heads might be later.

Analysis of finds, both of 'certain' and 'possible' grave-goods, gave some evidence that the north-turning heads had more Roman finds, that the ones near to 270° had fewer finds, and that the south-turning ones had more definite finds, including many of the knives. One of the **radiocarbon dates (ad 153)** belonged to the first group, consistent with a 'Roman' date, but another 'early' date **(ad 228) was in the last group,** which is rather counter to any idea that these are late. Neither the primary data on which the statistics were compiled, nor the home-made statistical techniques employed, were good enough to deal with complex associations of this kind. It was not possible, therefore, to assess the extent to which anomalous evidence was within limits of statistical error. Computerization of the data might have yielded (and perhaps still might yield) a more positive result.

A model was nevertheless postulated which, even if it rests on insecure foundations, may suggest the way in which research on this type of cemetery might develop, given comparative data from more complete and better-recorded sites. Taking into account other evidence outlined above, a three-phase grouping could be suggested, of which the first two groups were really one continuing cemetery with respect for existing graves, and the third diverging in orientation and possibly superimposed on the earlier pattern. The three phases may be 'interpreted historically' as follows:

A: Pagan cemetery of north-turning heads with some Roman grave-goods associated with a Roman shrine or mausoleum which might be primary or secondary; ? 2nd to ? 6th centuries AD?

B: Christian phase of near-270° orientated graves few or no finds, associated with a nucleus of a 'holy' grave (who was the girl?) which became a focus of pilgrimage; ?6th-?7th centuries AD.

C: Semi-Christian phase, heads moving to south, more grave-goods, especially knives, possibly representing the movement into the area of pagan or semi-converted English; ?7th-?8th centuries.

Clearly if such a model could be maintained on a scientific basis, it would be of the greatest historical interest. The frightening aspect of this model is that it sounds so plausible, and there is great danger of it being swallowed uncritically, especially by historians, who like archaeological evidence that fits into an accepted 'historical framework'. The usefulness of such a 'historical' model is not whether it is 'true' (though I think there are elements of truth in it) but whether it provides a useful base from which to consider the character of other cemeteries in this class, and the kind of analysis that is needed. Alternative models (especially related to the evidence of multi-nuclear development) would also be desirable, especially ones which did not seek to explain the phasing in a 'historical' way, but more in terms that would be acceptable to an archaeologist of the second millennium BC or of American Indians. An open mind must be preserved, and multiple models are the best way of ensuring this, as has been demonstrated with regard to the equally difficult problem of hillfort re-occupation. A model need not be a constricting straitjacket, as the single pre-excavation military model of South Cadbury proved to be, and as seemed to be implied by an archaeologist talking at a recent conference about his site: 'We have not built up any models; we're keeping all options open'!

The cemetery evidence posed problems about its relationship to the local settlement pattern, in which there are three main constituents:

1 An adjacent highly defensible hillfort, with evidence of Roman and/or later occupation and possible new defences.

2 A Roman 'town', Combwich, of which little is known as its features are buried deeply in silt. It lies close to the River Parrett, at the end of a Roman road from Ilchester, possibly a port for the Somerset hinterland (? ISCALIS). Combwich was reached by a ford across the Parrett from the end of the road, and marks the limit of intensive Romanization in Somerset almost as decisively as does Exeter in Devon. The Quantocks and Exmoor seem to have inhibited any substantial development in this direction, even on the coastal strip towards Minehead.

3 The nearby village of Cannington is a 'typical' valley settlement, certainly in existence by the earlier 11th century, and very likely dating from the period of English settlement which in this area is likely to be in the later 7th or 8th century; there is, however, a little Roman pottery from Cannington village.

It is tempting, of course, to relate the cemetery to the adjoining hillfort settlement; the size of the cemetery would indicate a population of 100+, certainly more than an extended family, and appropriate to a hillfort settlement. If this is true, the hillfort occupation extended well back into the Roman period. Was it even the conventional 're-occupation'; did the prehistoric settlement ever die out? Are the prehistoric finds on the cemetery site evidence that the cemetery is of Iron Age origin? The presence of two Beakers (found before controlled excavation) points to an even earlier use. There are indeed a number of graves which could be prehistoric, i.e. where no Roman finds give a *terminus post quem*. If this could be proved (e.g. by radiocarbon dating), Cannington, and perhaps other cemeteries of the class discussed in this paper, might have their origins in the Iron Age or earlier.

Was Combwich specifically the port of this settlement, or was it a separate settlement? Was there a gradual shift from its site to the more secure hilltop one? Flooding and piratical threats may have made it increasingly untenable, especially after the middle of the 4th century.

The origins of the cemetery in relation to the hillfort and Combwich can be further explored by excavation particularly in the hillfort and the earthworks on its southern slopes, which are still open ground at the time of writing.

The reasons for the ending of the cemetery may be more easily ascertained. Hilltop settlement as a phenomenon is not characteristic of the English settlement and that of the Cannington hillfort area can hardly have remained viable for more than a generation or two after the English became politically dominant in south-west Somerset. One can envisage a situation parallel to that of the 1st century, with English Cannington gradually becoming the economic and social focus of the area, and establishing its own Christian church and cemetery. The latest graves in our cemetery could be that of the earliest English settlers being absorbed into the existing socio-economic structure, or they may be the graves of the last of the indigenous inhabitants, far removed from *Romanitas* and perhaps even the first flush of Christian conversion, and making increasing cultural contact with the newcomers, until they were finally absorbed by it.

Notes

1 But not all: Brown cites the north-south Christian graves at Hartlepool, and many others could be quoted from medieval and modern contexts.

2 e.g. to face the resurrection; the east-west orientation said to be given to priests is to enable them to face their west-east flocks.

3 See now Baillie Young, *Merovingian Funeral Rites and the Evolution of Christianity: a Study in the historical interpretation of archaeological material* (PhD, University of Pennsylvania 1975)

4 Except for revised $^{12}C/^{13}C$ ratio, which makes them significantly different from the dates already published in *Radiocarbon* and the CBA list.

Table I *Roman and later west-east cemeteries with sparse finds: a sample list*

Site name	Location	County	Context	No. of Graves	Est. Orig. No.	?Coffins	Orient.	Attitude	Grave goods	Date claimed	Dating evidence	Special features	References (Brit = Britannia)
Ancaster	West cemetery	Lincs.	Roman town	91	—	few stone few nails	W-E 94% excl. 12 infants	most extended 1 crouch 1 prone	few	late	TPQ early IV	rows, claimed Christian, pagan slabs used as coffin lids	Wilson 1968
Banwell	road to Worle	Som.	by road	many	—	—	W-E	—	Roman coins? brooch?			'wounds'	Knight 1902, 458
Beacon Hill		Oxon.	none	34	—	—	—	—	—	late or post-Roman	TPQ late RB pot	found in motorway	Brit 4 (1973), 296
Blaise Castle		Glos.	?Roman ?temple	6+	many		W-E except one		?late	?late Roman	coin of mid IV below bones	many in earlier excavations	Rahtz and Brown 1959
Bletsoe		Beds.	margin of Roman site	40		nails, cists	NW-SE		v.few	late Roman	TPQ IV	earlier gullies on grave alignment	Brit 2 (1971), 267 Med Archaeol 16 (1972), 147
Bradley Hill		Som.	IV homestead	26	?26	stone-lined + one stone coffin	W-E, few N-S		few	Roman ?plus		secondary to earlier group of 23 inside building, SW-NE, with coins of III and IV in mouth	Brit 1 (1970), 296 Brit 4 (1973), 310-11 inf. R Leech
Bray		Berks.	settlement by R. Thames							V	pot of c. 420-50, TAQ of c.470-520		Brit 3 (1972), 349
Brean Down	sand cliff	Som.	Roman temple + on hill above dated into V	many		limestone blocks by one	?W-E	?extended	1 knife "triangular"		14C date centres in VI	mostly destroyed without record	ApSimon et al. 1961, 86, 120-22, 125-27; 14C date corrected from that in Radiocarbon and CBA list
Caerwent	Vicarage garden	Mon.	outside gate of Roman town	118+	118+	stone cists: one wooden coffin in stone cist	W-E	varying	one iron bracelet	post-Roman		cemetery overlay late Roman features; 14C dates in V, VI, VIII, IX	Archaeology in Wales 13 (CBA Group 2, 1973) (see Archaeologia 12 1911); 14C dates Harwell 493-7

Table I (continued)

Site name	Location	County	Context	No. of Graves	Est. Orig. No.	?Coffins	Orient.	Attitude	Grave goods	Date claimed	Dating evidence	Special features	References (Brit = Britannia)
Camerton		Som.	outside Roman town	109	?109			various	many, but many without	'Saxon' VII	Finds of IV, V, VI, VII	claimed as Christian by Hyslop	See Rahtz and Fowler 1972, 200 with refs
Cannington		Som.	on hill by hillfort	523 individuals	2000-5000	lining slabs	W-E within 55° either side of 270°	most extended 3 crouched	few, mostly knives	?II-?VIII	14C date and grave goods II-VIII VII-VIII	2 nuclei, one on hilltop may be ?temple, other a slab-marked grave with path leading to it	Rahtz monograph in prep.
Cirencester	between SE gate and amphith.	Glos.	Roman town	150		1 stone				?Roman	one coin of Honorius	1 with 120 bootnails	*Brit* 1 (1970) 293 *Brit* 3 (1972) 339 see now McWhirr 1973, 195-200
Daw's Castle		Som.	cliff-edge earthwork	'numbers'			W-E						Page 1890, 241-2
Doulting		Som.		6			W-E					?in row	Gray 1925, 114-6
Dorchester		Oxon.	Roman town	78 dug, 200 seen	700+	27 with nails and fittings	W-E with variation	extended	none	IV-VI	14C date centres in V	rect. enclosure 110 x 120m N-S stakeholes	Durham and Rowley 1972
Eccles		Kent	outside SE corner of villa	large number						sub or post-Roman		relevant to place-name ?	*Brit* 2 (1971) 288 *Brit* 3 (1972), 351
Eccleston		Ches.	near Roman building	20	20+		W-E		none	post-Roman		all male	inf. J D Bu'Lock
Frilford		Berks.	near temple									A/S cemetery close by	*Antiq Journ* 1 (1921), 87-97 *Oxoniensia* 4 (1939), 54-55; 5 (1940), 166-7
Henley Wood		Som.	secondary to Roman temple through ruins and extending to east	50	50-100		W-E	extended	none	?late Roman	Roman residual; VI, if of settlement of Cadbury Congresbury	some double	*Journ Rom Stud* 53 (1963) 146; 55 (1965), 216; *Brit* 1 (1970), 296; inf. E Greenfield
Icklingham		Suff.	near Roman building				W-E		coin and bracelets	IV		Christian lead tank nearby	*Brit* 6 (1975), 262
King's Weston Down	Henbury	Glos.	near hillfort	10+	10+		W-E	extended	none	V-VII?	TPQ Iron Age pot	?could be Iron age	Godman 1972

Table I (continued)

Site name	Location	County	Context	No. of Graves	Est. Orig. No.	?Coffins	Orient.	Attitude	Grave goods	Date claimed	Dating evidence	Special features	References (Brit = Britannia)
Knockea	Knockea Hill	Limerick	inside enclosure	66	66		W-E	extended	none			stout posts in encl. bank ditch outside	O'Kelly 1967
Lamyatt Beacon		Som.	north of temple	12	12+		W-E to SW-NE	extended	none				pers. comm. R Leech
Llandegai		Caerns.	near henge monuments	c. 50		trace	W-E	no bones	none			3 rows, rect. feature with off centre grave	Houlder 1968
Llantwit Major		Glam.	cutting villa mosaics	many			W-E				later than villa		*Archaeol Camb* **102** (1953), 89-163; *Brit* **3** (1972), 300
Lundy	Beacon Hill	Bristol Channel	enclosed cemetery	many			W-E			V	inscribed stone V+; seal III-IV pot	other ?early graves elsewhere on island	Gardner c. 1970 *Current Archaeol* **8** (May 1968), 196-202; **16** (Sept. 1969), 138-142; *Brit* **1** (1970) 297
Maiden Castle		Dorset	hillfort Roman temple	4?+1	5+		W-E	extended		IV	New Forest sherd in grave fill		Wheeler 1943, 77-8, pls. III, V
Monkwear-mouth/Jarrow		Durham	Saxon monasteries			wood coffins				?pre-VII	2 contained Roman pot	antedate earliest definably monastic structures	Cramp 1969, espec. 33, 45 *Med Archaeol* **16** (1972), 150
Portishead		Som.		43			W-E				residual ?IV pot	not on hill	*Archaeol Review* **4** (1969), 51
Poundbury		Dorset	below hill-fort and outside Roman town	4		wood coffins				sub- or post- Roman		secondary to Christian cemetery of IV; inside enclosure	see elsewhere in this publication: *Brit* **1** (1970), 298-9 *Brit* **2** (1971), 280-1 *Brit* **3** (1972), 345-6 *Brit* **4** (1973), 315-6 *Med Archaeol* **17** (1973), 138

Table I (continued)

Site name	Location	County	Context	Graves	Est. No.	?Coffins	Orient.	Attitude	Grave goods	Date claimed	Dating evidence	Special features	References (Brit = Briannia)
Stretton-on-the-Fosse		Warks.	near Roman buildings and in same field as A/S cemetery	4			W-E					beginnings of rows; secondary to 'boot' cemetery of 13 graves	Brit **3** (1972), 319; West Midlands Archaeol Newsletter **14** (1971), 22
Weston-S-Mare	S slopes below Worlesbury Hill	Som.	below hillfort	40-50								Material in Weston Museum; 'dry stone enclosures'	Proc Bath Nat Hist and Field Club **3** (1877), 395 ff
Welton Wold		Yorks. ER	villa site								later than late IV		Brit **3** (1972), 311
Weycock Hill	SE of temple	Berks.	temple plus settlement	30+	30+	one lead with coin and brick	W-E	extended	coin in coffin	—	—	shallow; spread over one acre	Cotton 1956-7, 55, 55, with refs
Winchester	Victoria Rd.			55		two	W-E earlier phases		few	Plate IV		latest group, varied orientation; 2 double graves each with coffin burial below uncoffined	Brit **4** (1973), 318
Wint Hill	Banwell	Som.	villa site	?50	?100+		W-E				later than IV		J Axbridge Caving Group and Archaeol Soc 1963, 35-42; 1964, 26-28; Knight 1902, 461

Bibliography

ApSimon, A M, Donovan, D T, and Taylor, H (1961) 'The stratigraphy and archaeology of the late-glacial and post-glacial deposits at Brean Down, Somerset' *Proc. Univ. Bristol Spelaeol. Soc.* **9,** 67-136

ApSimon, A M (1965) '**The Roman temple, Brean Down, Somerset**' *ibid.* **10,** 195-258

Barley, M W, and Hanson, R P C (eds) (1968) *Christianity in Britain, 300-700* (Leicester: University Press)

Brothwell, D (1972) 'Palaeodemography and earlier British populations' *World Archaeol.* **4,** 75-87

Brown, G Baldwin (1915) *The Arts in Early England,* vol. 3 (London: Murray)

Cotton, M A (1956-7) 'Weycock Hill, 1953' *Berkshire Archaeol. J* **55,** 48-68

Cramp, R (1969) 'Excavations at . . . Wearmouth and Jarrow . . .' *Medieval Archaeol.* **13,** 21-66

Durham, B, and Rowley, R T (1972) 'A cemetery site at Queensford Mill, Dorchester' *Oxoniensia* **37,** 32-7

Fowler, P J (1971) 'Hill-forts, AD 400-700' in Jesson and Hill 1961

Fowler, P J (ed) (1972) *Archaeology and the Landscape* (London: Baker)

Fowler, P J, Gardner, K S, and Rahtz, P A (1970) *Cadbury-Congresbury, Somerset, 1968* (Bristol: University)

Gardner, K S (ND-c. 1970) *Lundy, an Archaeological Field Trust* (Landmark Trust)

Gejvall, N G (1960) *Westerhus: Medieval Population and Church in the Light of Skeletal Remains* (Lund: KVHAA)

Gejvall, N G (1968) 'Early medieval church at Westerhus in the light of C14 collagen datings' in Martensson 1968, 136-40

Godman, C (1972) 'Kings Weston Hill, Bristol . . .' *Proc. Univ. Bristol Spelaeol. Soc.* **13,** 41-8

Gray, H St G (1925) 'Discovery of human skeletons at Doulting, Somerset' *Proc. Somerset Archaeol. Natur. Hist. Soc.* **71,** 114-6

Houlder, C H (1968) 'The henge monuments at Llandegai' *Antiquity* **42,** 216-21

Hyslop, M (1963) 'Two Anglo-Saxon cemeteries at Chamberlain's Barn, Leighton Buzzard, Bedfordshire' *Archaeol. J* **120,** 161-200

Jesson, M, and Hill, D (1971) *The Iron Age and its Hillforts* (Southampton: University)

Johnson, W (1912) *Byways in British Archaeology* (Cambridge: University Press)

Knight, F A (1902) *The Sea-board of Mendip* (London: Dent)

McWhirr, A D (1973) 'Cirencester, 1969-72; 9th Interim Report' *Antiq. J* **53,** 191-218

Martensson, A (ed) (1968) *Res Medievales* (Lund)

Meaney, A L, and Hawkes, S C (1970) 'Two Anglo-Saxon cemeteries at Winnall' *Soc. Medieval Archaeol. Monograph* **4**

O'Kelly, M J (1967) 'Knockea, Co. Limerick' in Rynne, E (ed) *North Munster Studies,* 72-101

OS *Map of Dark Age Britain* (1966) (Chessington: Ordnance Survey)

Page, J L W (1890) *An Exploration of Exmoor* (London)

Ramm, H G et al (1971) 'The tombs of . . . Gray and . . . Ludham . . . in York Minster . . .' *Archaeologia* **103,** 101-47

Rahtz, P A (1957) 'King's Weston Down Camp, Bristol, 1956' *Proc. Univ. Bristol Spelaeol. Soc.* **8,** 30-8

Rahtz, P A (1968) 'Sub-Roman cemeteries' in Barley and Hanson 1968, 193-5

Rahtz, P A (1970) 'Excavations on Glastonbury Tor, Somerset, 1964-6' *Archaeol. J* **127,** 1-81

Rahtz, P A (1973) 'Monasteries as settlements' *Scot. Archaeol. Forum* **5,** 125-35

Rahtz, P A, and Brown, J C (1959) 'Blaise Castle Hill, Bristol, 1957' *Proc. Univ. Bristol Spelaeol. Soc.* **8,** 147-71

Rahtz, P A, and Fowler, P J (1972) 'Somerset AD 400-700' in Fowler ed. 1972, 187-221

Rahtz, P A, and Hirst, S (1974) *Beckery Chapel, Glastonbury 1967-8* (Glastonbury: Antiquarian Society)

Salin, E (1952) *La Civilisation Mérovingienne,* **2** (Paris: Picard)

Struever, S (ed) (1971) 'Approaches to the social dimensions of mortuary practices' *Mem. Soc. Amer. Archaeol.* **25**

Thomas, C (1971), *The Early Christian Archaeology of North Britain* (London: OUP)

Toynbee, J M C (1971) *Death and Burial in the Roman World* (London: Thames and Hudson)

Ucko, P J (1969) 'Ethnography and archaeological interpretation of funerary remains' *World Archaeol.* **1,** 262-77

Wheeler, R E M (1943) *Maiden Castle, Dorset* (London: Society of Antiquaries Res. Rep. **12**)

Wilson, D R (1968) 'An early Christian cemetery at Ancaster' in Barley and Hanson 1968, 196-9

Index

65